Crazy

Graham Jones

ARROW BOOKS

Arrow Books Limited
62–65 Chandos Place, London WC2N 4NW

An imprint of Century Hutchinson Limited

London Melbourne Sydney Auckland
Johannesburg and agencies throughout the world

First published 1987

Phototypeset by Input Typesetting Ltd, London
Printed and bound in Great Britain by
Anchor Brendon Limited, Tiptree, Essex

ISBN 0 09 954400 8

Contents

Acknowledgements 5

I Hereby Name This Book . . . 7
Boats, Boats, Boats 16
Ocean Greats 32
Celebrity Salts 50
(Fool?) Hardy Amateurs 66
Floating Capital 83
Making Waves 100
Freshwater Interlude 114
Boat Crazy 127
Useful Phrases – A Landlubber-Old Salt Translator 146

About the author 159

Acknowledgements

Firstly, a 'hip hip hip' to Peter Lavery and Francesca Liversidge at Arrow Books for coming up with the basic idea for this book and navigating me successfully through the project.

The eventual product might well have been scuppered if it was not for the very kind help I had from all manner of celebrity sailors and sailing celebrities. Their keeness to assist and readiness to provide material showed just what affection boats engender, from the biggest yacht to the humblest dinghy.

I would like to thank, most profoundly, for giving up their time to share their best boat memories:

Greg Barnes; Raymond Baxter, FRSA; Bill Beaumont, OBE; Robert Bedlow; Jill Bennett; Jim Bowen; Alistair Buchan; Ray Bulman; Mike Burns; John Carter; Peter Cumberlidge; Brenda Dean; Jonathan Dimbleby; the Earl of Dundonald; Sir Ranulph Fiennes, Bt; Richard V. Giordano; John Hannam, MP; Robert Holmes; Ralph Hammond Innes, CBE; Jeremy Irons; Dame Naomi James, DBE; Robin Knox-Johnston CBE; the Krankies (Ian and Janette Tough); Sir Maurice Laing; Syd Little; William Lucas; Lulu; Norris McWhirter, CBE; Philip Madoc; Lewis Malandrone; Richard Mayne; Leif Mills; Dame Alison Munro, DBE; Sir Edwin Nixon; Basil D'Oliveira; Geoff Pack; John Ridgway;

Brent Sadler; Des Sleightholme; Ewen Southby-Tailyour, OBE; Dick Taverne, QC; Venerable William Thomas; Malcolm Thornton, MP; Sir Leslie Young, CBE, DL.

When quoting other yachting works I have tried to give the source, including author and publisher: anyone who feels omitted is invited to contact the publisher for inclusion in future editions.

I must also thank the publishers of Britain's national and Sunday newspapers, whose reports on the more amusing side of life afloat form the basis for this book: and all at the *Daily Telegraph* library.

Special gratitude to Mike Peyton for supplying the cartoons.

Thanks are also due to my wife Lynne (no mere 'sexist' reference to efforts in the galley but for playing her part as a full member of the crew as far as research went). Fortunately we only got into heavy water once or twice during what has been, overwhelmingly, a very happy voyage into the humorous side of boats everywhere.

I Hereby Name This Book . . .

'People,' said the famous Sea Lord, 'fall into three categories. Those who are thinking about buying a boat, people who are buying a boat, and those who are baling one out.'

All the world loves a boat lover, in the words of the popular sea shanty (was it Jerome Kerne or Jerome K. Jerome?), and it is not difficult to see why.

From the mega-gin palace down to the humblest

Sir Edwin Nixon

Chairman and former chief executive, IBM United Kingdom

Most amusing moment
The Norfolk Broads: late forties, at a time when yachts were well in the majority. Tacking up a narrow river against a headwind, a motor cruiser, after several attempts to get by, finally made it. As he passed with much accelerating, a voice from the cruiser shouted: 'Can't you make up your b***** mind about which direction to take?' (An actual happening!)

---

dinghy, boats are graced with sleek, evocative lines, the promise of escape from mundanity and the certainty of adventure – just feel the spray in your nostrils. Why else do they always figure in after-shave commercials, James Bond films, and half the cartoons in the *Sunday Express*?

Boating men, are as we know, totally masculine, healthy, rugged and adventurous. They also like to wear a beard and mess about with engines. I will not make the obvious joke that boating women are, of course, exactly the same. Indeed, most women in the sailing world I have come across are extremely glamorous creatures, which has no doubt aided the popular image of what people (sic) do in boats. (Apart from being . . .) (sic).

'Sailing people,' said the famous Sea Lord, 'fall into three categories. Those who love their boats, those who want to love their boats, and those who love *in* their boats.'

A little more of this later, though it must be said that sex is not a compulsory part of sailing and often a very uncomfortable one too. PVC on PVC might excite some but otherwise produces the most unhappy squelching noises. In calm waters (e.g., harbours) it also has the side-effect of literally making waves. (If you landlubbers don't believe me stand on any quayside at night and watch for the ebb and flow of that telltale rhythmic rippling!)

That is why if you are looking in this compendium for lots of tales of Fiona Richmond-style capers you will be disappointed, I am afraid. The favoured stories swapped between old (and new) salts in quayside bars and clubrooms usually concern 1) near misses, 2) the mistakes of fellow adventurers, 3) the heads (toilets to you landlubbers), 4) the

Jeremy Irons

International film and TV star

First boating memory

All my life I have been around boats in one form or another and have, I hope sensibly, a healthy respect for water and thank heavens have not experienced too many occasions of great fear.

I remember, however, going along with my brother when I was aged about nine to inspect his lobster pots off Bembridge Ledge on the Isle of Wight. We motored the half-mile out to sea in our clinker-built launch, towing the dinghy behind. On reaching the Ledge Buoy, which tolled mournfully and heaved in and out of the water, I watched my brother and his friend transfer into the dinghy. This left me alone in the launch moored to this bleak, barnacle encrusted monster. I was not unhappy to be marooned thus, yet remember looking forward to their return as I watched them proceed up the line of pots some fifty yards between me and the shore.

Suddenly, the water to the seaward side began to grow into a huge wave which broke into white foam as a black monster broke the surface and sped by me. My panic at this eruption was quickly tempered by the oncoming problem of keeping the launch upright as its wash passed me.

To a nine-year-old this surprise close encounter with a submarine made an indelible impression!

heads (toilets to you landlubbers) and 5) the heads (toilets to you landlubbers).

Come to think of it, much the same as air-traffic controllers and air stewardesses talk about when they are resting on land, which is a cue to talk about my previous work *Plane Crazy* which charted the heady exploits of the flying community.

As with my previous tome, in the preparation of this volume I have been assisted by a formidable battery of celebrity talent who now have been persuaded to unleash on an unsuspecting public their favourite tales of boats. The willingness and the fervour to contribute which many famous sailors showed speaks I think for both the passion and the comradeship the yachting world engenders: e.g., Bill Beaumont, English rugby union captain turned 'Question of Sport' skipper who told me, 'after running aground last year I had to take a lot of

Robin Knox-Johnston

World-record-breaking single-handed yachtsman

First sailing memory

I was four years old and had made a raft out of bits and pieces of an orange box. I carried it down to the Dee and launched it, and then climbed on board. The raft sank, even with my slight weight. An early introduction to the Archimedes Principle!

Favourite sailing anecdote

In 1969, after I had sailed around the world, I was the guest of the Elder Brethren of Hull Trinity

House, a group of remarkably bright eighty-year-olds, broad of shoulder and white of head, who had all held command of sailing ships. One approached me and said: 'Well, young man, what was the weather like when you rounded Cape Horn?'

I was embarrassed. 'Well, sir,' I replied, 'I am, er afraid, that I was, er flat becalmed.'

The white bushy eyebrows lowered, and two clear blue eyes looked at me. 'Don't you go telling people about that then,' he said. 'You'll ruin our image.'

Best sailing memory

Sitting alongside Mylor Quay in 1968, waiting to be floated off by the tide, about five days before I set off around the world. An 'expert' came up, followed by a group of tourists. You can always tell an expert by their rig. Submariners sweater, reefer jacket, white trousers tucked into sea boots with socks rolled down over the top, and, of course, a white yachting cap. He looked down at *Suhaili* and said, 'Where be you going in that?' I replied that I was thinking of heading towards Australia.

'What in this, it'll never get to Australia. Whose going with you?' I explained that I was going alone, which brought forth the question 'What you going to do at nights then?' I pointed proudly to my rather bulky self-steering, and explained that this apparatus would steer the boat. He asked if it worked, and I had to admit that I had not tried it as yet. 'It won't work,' he said. Then after a short pause. 'You be careful around Land's End.'

stick from my friends. One sent me an exam paper in maritime navigation.'

I particularly liked the reply to my question 'What is the most exciting thing to happen to you afloat?' offered by one famous name (not Bill): five exclamation marks!

It is a rather large world too – three million people each weekend messing about in boats around our coast or on our inland waterways, many of them new to the sport, and encouraged by the dynamic exploits of Dennis Conner in the America's Cup; perhaps the even more dynamic ones of supersolo sailor Lynne in BBC's 'Howard's Way'; or perhaps it is because the City has gone mad about flotations.

My own extremely limited what-passed-for-a-sailing-bug was much nurtured by television. I don't think it was so much 'Captain Pugwash' or news film of Edward Heath at the helm of *Morning Cloud* but rather the thrills and spills of the Cod War. What really clinched it I suspect was the thrill of Cubs (dyb, dyb, dyb) and learning all those exciting knots.

Three million afloat leaves some fifty-three million at home watching 'Opportunity Knocks' (remember friends, it's your boats that count) which is according to your fancy 1) room for improvement, 2) a clever deception since there are clearly fifty-five million people jammed onto the Norfolk Broads every Sunday or 3) all the landlubbers deserve.

For my part I hope this book will fall into the hands of some of the fifty-three million non-sailors (all fifty-three million of them would be quite good for sails, not to mention sales, in fact) so they can learn of what they are missing. I would not be too upset if any of them could not tell a Brigantine from a Thames dredger, or thought bilge was something politicians talked, a coaster was a drinks mat and a rubber dinghy was a device aimed at preventing the spread of AIDS.

Mind you, as the famous Sea Lord said to me: 'People fall into three categories. They are either climbing into boats, thinking of climbing into boats – or falling out of them.'

I hope all of you enjoy the book.

Graham Jones

Jill Bennett

Cinema and stage actress

[Jill Bennett was with the famous classical actor, Godfrey (later Sir Godfrey) Tearle for four years, and wrote a moving book in his memory. She recalled how he had accepted, in lieu of salary for a major part in the film *One of Our Aircraft is Missing*, the boat *Barbara Mary*: one day she was invited aboard.]

I wasn't allowed to hang about at Messack Point over breakfast. I was hurried, clumping, down the rocky path dressed in full Cornish seaman's gear. Godfrey had bought it for me before I arrived. There were thick oiled wool sweaters, oilskins, gumboots, and a real sou'wester. I looked like an old-fashioned advertisement for Halibut Liver Oil.

He rowed me out to the *Barbara Mary* in the dinghy, and we climbed on board. I hadn't set foot on deck two minutes before I found that my role had changed. I was no longer the welcomed guest, ▶

the girl he was fond of and whom he enjoyed spoiling and chatting to, the one who made him laugh, I was the cabin boy (a role I was later to play in the Alan Ladd film *Hell Below Zero*).

Godfrey rapped out instructions as he hoisted the sails, looked across at me and expected me to jump to it. I was given the job of sluicing the deck with a mop. So I washed the deck, and polished the woodwork until it was so bright it looked positively vulgar.

When we set off to sail up river my role changed again; I was ordered to put away the mop and become first mate. I'd sailed a bit in Cornwall as a child, and also on a loch when I was at school in Scotland, but I'd forgotten everything I knew, including every word of the vocabulary. I didn't know that a rope was a sheet, I had no idea what a painter was, and I was inclined to argue.

'Never argue with the Captain,' snapped Godfrey.

He wasn't joking.

The autumn gales had begun in Cornwall and it often poured with rain. These were the equinoctial gales which can be very fierce, and when the wind was strong the waves were huge and thundered onto the beach, making the *Barbara Mary* rock wildly and tug at her mooring.

When the storms died down, off we went in the boat up river to Truro. The sun shone, and the fields and woods looked peaceful, but the water had a powerful swell and the boat heaved. I hadn't been on board for half an hour before I began to feel very sick. I was given to sea-sickness, car-sickness, everything-sickness, and I had sensibly packed anti-seasick tablets in my suitcase. Determined not to lose face with the Captain, whether I was cabin boy or mate, I secretly took two of the tablets before we set off. No good. The motion of the boat was relentless. I had to creep down to the kitchen (which Godfrey said I must call the galley) to be sick in decent privacy. On almost every trip we took, although I enjoyed it, I was sick. I was pleased with myself for hiding this. It was quite a coup to be sick and then manage to get back on deck looking unconcerned. One night at home, after a glass of champagne at dinner, I suddenly confessed.

'I want to tell you something,' I blurted out. 'I know you haven't noticed, and I didn't mean to let you know. But it does seem rather stupid to go on pretending. I keep getting seasick, and creeping down to the kitch . . . – sorry, galley – to be sick.'

Godfrey looked astounded. Then began to laugh. I was rather offended. Being sick wasn't as funny as all that. Then, still laughing, he told me that *he* was seasick too. He'd been taking the same tablets. I had bought mine in London, he had gone to Truro for his. When I wasn't in the galley – he had always presumed I was making coffee or cutting the sandwiches – he had taken the chance to go down and be sick too. Both of us, it seemed, had been determined not to disgrace ourselves.

Reprinted from *Godfrey: A Special Time Remembered*, Jill Bennett (Hodder and Stoughton, 1983) with the author's permission.

Boats, Boats, Boats

The first thing to remember about a boat is that to get maximum use out of it, it should float. This may seem elementary, but occasionally is overlooked by those buying a vessel for the first time. (A boat which does not float is known as a wreck).

Some other golden rules of the road for new mariners (experienced salts may skip this bit):

1. Alcohol and water don't mix.
2. Baked beans though simple to simmer are *not* the most convenient food in a confined space.
3. Try to start with something under 70ft.
4. Mud up the name of your boat so nobody can report your nautical outrages.
5. Until you've got the hang of it, don't try anything too adventurous, e.g., smuggling £5 million of heroin, gun-running to Honduras, a race to Kharg Island and back before tea.

You should also be careful what you call your boat. It should not be named after a current fancy of less than ten years' standing or it may upset your eventual girlfriend/wife/husband. Nor should it be named after happy memories, e.g., *Flighty Barmaid III* or *That Night in Cleethorpes V*, or defy sailing superstitions, e.g., *Bermuda Triangle II, Mary Celeste III, The Incredible Hulk, The Titanic.*

Jim Bowen

Comedian and star of ITV's 'Bullseye!'

My sailing life
My boat is moored on Lake Windermere, which is just a short journey from home. Phyllis and I go out in it as often as possible, but we're far from being flash. In fact, we changed our first rather fast boat for a cabin cruiser and we just chug up and down the lake. Mind you, folk get to know who you are, and we've had more than one curious tourist cruising past and having a peep inside the cabin. Phyllis and I always have a good laugh, because we're sure they expect us to be knocking back the champagne. I'll never forget the look on one man's face as he came alongside and caught us doing our favourite thing – sitting in the cabin eating thick bacon-butties and swigging tea! It's our idea of the perfect bit of Bully on a Sunday afternoon.

You will need certain items of equipment, e.g., distress flares, aspirins, alka seltzer, a splint for broken arms and legs, a bucket for baling out, a copy of *Ring of Bright Water*, an assortment of bottles to put messages in, and the lyrics of 'Mud, Glorious Mud.'

One special word of warning, a 17ft boat is too small for a helipad.

If you are in a canoe, you may shoot rapids. Otherwise, do not shoot 1) albatrosses, 2) customs men or 3) your crew.

Always leave word with someone where you are going, unless you are married and not to your fellow sailor in which case that would defeat the whole object.

Two final golden rules:

1. 'Extremely spacious' as used by yacht brokers is just one of their little jokes.
2. If the hull doesn't leak, you can bet the cabin will.

And remember traditional greetings to the fellow sailor are:

1. What the h*** do you think you're doing?
2. Water, you imbecile.
3. Where did you learn to sail, the local dodgems?
4. How much did they pay you to take that hulk off their hands?

The largest-ever vessel blown from her moorings

Just to satisfy that it can happen to the best – and biggest – of 'em, in August 1985 the pride of the Fleet, aircraft carrier *Ark Royal* was prised from her moorings by 50 m.p.h. winds during visitors' day at Portland Navy Base, Dorset. Two Navy tugs were called to nudge the 19,500-ton carrier back to the quayside in the nearest thing to ignominy, RN.

First boat owner overtaken on a trunk road by his own yacht

A Royal Navy Commander had the shock of his life in April 1985 as he drove his Land-Rover across the Tamar Bridge. He happened to glance sideways out of the window . . . and saw, to his horror, his own 28ft yacht overtaking him. It had slipped the towbar and gathered speed on the downhill slope of the bridge.

Fortunately no one was hurt as the speedaway sloop smashed into an oncoming Mini and a Chevette. The boat was, unfortunately, wrecked.

First Ford Cortina to sail solo under its own power across the Irish Sea

This may sound like a tale that springs from too much of the famous Liffey brew, but indeed a Ford Cortina did cast herself adrift in February 1987, journeying 100 miles from Aberporth in West Wales before she was spotted by a merchant skipper four miles south of the Isle of Man.

Once they had satisfied themselves it was not a hoax, the coastguards then considered whether it was a job for the AA or the Royal Navy. They chose the Navy who brought in the minesweeper *HMS Bronington* to destroy the errant Ford with explosives. (Order: 'Sink the Cortina!')

The Cortina mounted on four buoys, had, inquiries revealed, been RN property in the first place, used as a target for missile practice, but had unfortunately broken loose and motored away across the Irish Sea all on its own. (And it hadn't even passed its MOT.)

Worst-ever harbour rampage by 'Dad's Navy'

First-time helmsmen may feel happy about this, but few could beat the havoc wreaked by the minesweeper *Killiekrankie*, manned by naval reservists, when in August 1975 it decided to exit from Great Yarmouth harbour. In the skirmish that followed one boat was sunk, two more were crushed, and a naked girl scrambled away screaming for her safety.

Alistair Buchan

Yachting enthusiast and writer

Sailing memory No. 1
There was the wet, windy night when we were going to Cadiz when lights by the thousand popped up over the horizon. It had to be the local fishing fleet coming in for the night. I wiped the rain from my spectacles and peered seawards.

'I think the first one's a warship,' I risked.

'Yes,' confirmed Leo who, as befitting his RN status, had the binos. I decided to push my luck.

'I think the second one's another warship.' (I liked using 'warship'. It sounded so professional and I was in the company of professionals.)

'Yes,' said Leo. 'You don't get many civilian aircraft carriers.'

Sailing memory No. 2
Never be late for Hull Marina. We were late arriving and looked everywhere for a berth to wait for the locks to open the next morning. But it was either risk drying out in the channel leading to the lock gates (a sewer surrounded by mud) or try anchoring in Hull Roads. We were counting the

The ocean-going sit-com occurred as the 'Dad's Navy' vessel left the quay to return to her base in Scotland after a courtesy visit.

Thwack! First the 350-ton *Killiekrankie* smashed beamwards into a 20ft sloop owned by Mike Wilson

---

votes for the lesser of the two evils when a figure appeared on the lock gates and cried: 'Wait there. I'll open the gates.'

Salvation! We could hardly believe our luck and hovered obediently in the middle of the channel. The water round the lock gates swirled as the sluice gates were raised and then, oh joy, the gates began to open.

I had turned round to cock the outboard into gear when I heard a gurgle of fear from John (who had gone forward to look after the bow rope when we entered the lock) as if someone had him by the throat. It was the sort of sound that instantly catches your attention and I still treasure the image of him kneeling in the bows facing forwards but looking back at me and pointing to the wall of water rushing at us from the still half-full lock!

The wave picked us up and threw us onto the mud, lingering just long enough to tempt me to leap over the side in an effort to push us back into the channel. By the time I was back aboard, covered in evil-smelling slime, our latter day Moses was once again standing on the lock gates surveying the downfall of yet another of the grotty yachties who plagued his life.

'That's you till tomorrow,' he cried and disappeared.

---

of New Zealand. It sank immediately.

Thud! Then a holiday cruiser was crushed, and almost with it naked Dutch holidaymaker Gaia Son. She scrambled out dishabille, to be assisted to safety in a state of shock. But that was not all. . . .

Crack! The minesweeper then hit a spanking new 25ft catamaran owned by Brian Smith and his wife. He said: 'I was having a cup of tea with my two crewmen when we heard this churning noise. We then saw the stern of the minesweeper coming towards us.'

Naval goodwill visits to the Norfolk holiday resort are plainly fraught with problems. In September 1970, carpenter John Negus, his wife Jennifer and four-month-old baby were enjoying a Norfolk Broads holiday when their boat was suddenly sunk by the minesweeper *Wolverton* after she had veered to port and struck two yachts. It was revealed that twenty-four hours earlier another naval auxiliary vessel had collided with two privately owned cruisers.

Best cautionary tale to stay away from steam power

I still have nightmares at a passage in Eric Hiscock's memorable work *Wandering Under Sail* (OUP, 1978). This concerned a tanker steaming into San Francisco. As she was berthing one of the line handlers on the wharf apparently called up to the officer on her fo'c's'le head: 'Say, what ya got there, bud?'

Reported Mr Hiscock sombrely: 'Looking over the starboard bow the officer saw with horror the mast and rigging of a sailing yacht hanging on the anchor in its hawsepipe.'

Worst traffic chaos caused by an ocean-going yacht

Or two ocean-going yachts, to be precise – *Mercedes III*, Australia's third place in the Fastnet, and her fellow racer *Caprice of Huon.*

It had been declared impossible to ship them from Plymouth to Australia for the next set of races, and their crews were on 'a refresher' before the next round of competition. So, in August 1967, it was decided that they should travel 220 miles by road, on two articulated lorries to London docks.

That is where it all went wrong – causing traffic chaos in the West Country for almost a week, and being dubbed 'the police's biggest-ever game of snakes and ladders.'

The racers were carefully routed one square backwards from Exeter to the South to avoid a low bridge. Then they advanced to Honiton where it had been calculated that at 15′ 6″, they would just pass under a railway bridge, 'Max Headroom', as they say on TV, 15′ 8″. But someone had got his measurements wrong, and the ocean racers proved two inches too high for the clearance.

Police decided they should go back another snakes and ladders square and be re-routed. But they proved too tall for yet another bridge. And as the 'forward one backwards three' game was being played out, all the while traffic was building up for one of the busiest holiday weekends of the year.

On the roads there was chaos. Exasperated police meanwhile announced the yachts were being sent back to try again: 'We are going to send them two squares south and advance them on the A35 towards Sidmouth, hoping we can reach Honiton that way.'

Police blamed the haulage firm for giving them the wrong measurements; the hauliers blamed the owners for poor calculations. Meanwhile the AA was furious and motorists, in scores of jams throughout the West Country, fumed.

The Australian crews, blissfully unaware of the jams, meanwhile flew back to their native land for what was described as 'a heroes welcome'. It was not known whether this was for the race itself, or for getting the better of so many 'poms'.

Mike Burns

Leading club dinghy enthusiast and writer

Favourite memory

Towards the end of a week's sailing course two of our young daughters were released by their mentor to sail 'solo' (for the first time) in a quiet area of Chichester harbour. All was going nervously well until there were some rather ominous gusts of wind. As if this weren't enough another boat appeared on the scene.

This was not just 'another boat', however. Its helm personified confidence, even arrogance, as he embarked on a series of extravagant tacks and gybes across a stretch of nearby empty water. To the girls it was as if Nijinsky had suddenly appeared at the Saturday morning ballet class.

Unfortunately at this point the wind freshened in earnest. Too late did the girls even begin to be

Ripest nautical language

Andrew Morton told in his book *The Royal Yacht Britannia* (Orbis, 1984) how on her visit to Hollywood and California, the Queen found she could not travel in her shipped black bullet-proof limousine because of a succession of storms and floods. The local roads were under four feet of water. Never one to disappoint her admirers, it was decided the monarch should travel, equipped with Wellington boots and brolly, in a navy bus. ▶

---

aware of the danger. Their boat heeled, altered course and, as if guided by an unseen hand, headed straight for the 'intruder'.

There was a confusion of conflicting commands, whirring blocks and flying sheets as the unthinkable became the distinctly possible. It was all to no avail. With a splintering crunch their bows smashed into the side of the other craft.

For a moment there was deathly silence. Then its helm, clearly beside himself with rage, scrambled to his feet, his lower half already beginning to disappear beneath the gurgling waters.

'What the **** do you think you're playing at?' he roared. Cathy's eyes, wide in her ashen face, focused on the faded bit of green ribbon tied to the shroud she was clutching.

'Starboard,' she said, falteringly.

When one of the Britannia's officers attempted to communicate this change of plan to his opposite number in the US Navy, he was met with incredulity. According to Mr Morton, choice Anglo-Saxon expletives were exchanged, but the British stiff upper lip won.

'Triumphantly the officer put down the phone and then, to his horror, realized the Queen had been listening. Blushing, he tried to stammer out an apology.

'But she smiled sweetly and said: "I've been married to a sailor of thirty-six years and I've heard it all before." '

Most misleading pilot

It is to be hoped that few took literally the sailing regulations displayed in English, at the Adriatic resort of Lido de Jesolo.

Mainly concerned with avoiding 'bothers to bathers', they included this gem:

'In tracts of sea where the special channels are not, departure and arival (sic) must be made crossing the sheet of water with a course perpendicular to the beach.'

Walk on water

There was much ceremony as Frenchman Reny Bricka was bid farewell from County Hall, London, in July 1985, on a novel expedition to Paris on aquatic skis, ostensibly allowing him to 'walk on water' across the English Channel.

After being presented with a special scroll to mark

this unique nautical – even biblical – departure, the French adventurer literally strode off for home.

Dear, dear. He was immediately holed by his own safety boat and tipped ignominiously into the Thames.

Peter Cumberlidge

Yachting journalist and leading enthusiast

Most unusual memory

We had reached coffee and cognac and moved out on to the terrace. From here we could look across the Rance to where *Stormalong* was anchored, her flickering riding lights now clearly visible.

I felt completely relaxed. We'd had an agreeable, gently-paced cruise so far – Guernsey, Sark, Jersey, across to Chausey and then down to St Malo. St Suliac was a favourite haunt, so we had come through the lock this morning and carried a light northerly the three miles up to the village. Now, after the excellent *fruits de mer* and *rôti de boeuf*, I could even contemplate with some amusement the last part of the trip. You see, we were on our way to a funeral.

Well, not exactly a funeral – more of a casting upon the waters. We'd had a phone call from France shortly before leaving Dartmouth. It was Annette, my favourite eccentric aunt. Her husband Francois Dupont had died recently as we knew. He was eighty-six years old, and was always affectionately known as Le Truc. ►

Le Truc loved the sea and had a small fishing boat with which he used to gather crabs and lobsters. He had come sailing with us several times. 'It was his last wish,' Annette told me, 'that his ashes be scattered in the sea off Paimpol, to mingle with the wrack and the oysters as it were. I wondered if you would mind . . . I mean it would be so much more ceremonial from an English yacht.'

On the appointed day the weather was fine, although there was a blustery wind from the northwest. We were up early, washing down the decks and making sure that everything was shipshape. We ate a hearty breakfast and dressed with unaccustomed care.

At 1000 precisely I caught sight of Annette rounding the corner by the Café du Port. Behind her came a procession of three, a piratical-looking youth sandwiched between two old men.

The line halted alongside. Annette handed me a small casket and I laid it on the coachroof. We then shook hands with each member of the cortège as they came aboard.

'*Un petit*?' I asked Annette. She nodded and I poured six tots of cognac. We raised our glasses.

'Le Truc,' I ventured, and the toast was echoed in guttural Breton. I seated our guests and started the engine, which I'd already warmed up. Then we cast off and moved slowly out of the basin.

Once clear of the entrance we hoisted sail and *Stormalong* was soon slipping seawards past the picture-book islet of Ile St Riom and the white pyramid of Denou. I followed the string of reefs out to Les Charpentiers, came about without tacking the jib, and we lay quietly hove-to on the port tack. I nodded to Annette, who had been holding the casket steady.

The youth and one old man now produced Breton pipes from a duffel bag and began to play. They were leading up to a song and the third mourner came in with a deep bass. I hoped the proceedings would be finished before we drew too close to the rocky Mets de Goelo on the far side of the bay.

The requiem came to an end. Annette stood up, book in hand, and, moving easily to the sea, recited a seamen's prayer. Then, as she started to open the casket, it struck me that I'd forgotten to tell her about throwing to leeward. I made a tentative gesture with my arm, but Annette was now fascinated by the contents of the small wooden box. Luckily there was a brief lull as she made her cast, but the last few grams of Le Truc didn't quite make it and blew back across the deck. Annette didn't seem to notice and I went below to refill the glasses.

'Le Truc!' The final toast, but as I raised the cognac to my lips I noticed some grit in the bottom of the glass, perhaps blown in through the open port. I remained impassive and downed in one with the rest, reflecting that Le Truc would no doubt have approved of being partly carried off in a good *Eau-de-vie.*

Reprinted from *Yachting Monthly*, October 1984, with the author's permission.

Ray Bulman

Leading powerboating journalist

Best powerboat story (1)
Business partner of a leading international offshore driver wants to purchase a fast cruiser to join the up-market boating scene. He asks for help with his choice.

'Shall I buy a Moonraker or a Fairey Huntsman?'

'A Moonraker is OK. Has lots of accommodation, but a Fairey is a better seaboat,' is my advice.

'A better seaboat . . . Explain what you mean.'

'Well, if you are caught out in a blow, the hull of the Fairey would be better in a rough sea.'

'A rough sea, dear boy. Where would I be in a rough sea?'

'Could happen coming back, say, from Cherbourg . . .' I say thoughtfully.

'Cherbourg! My dear boy what the hell would I be doing in Cherbourg?' is his patronizing response.

'If I want to go to France I drive to Heathrow and catch a plane to Nice.

'I am bringing Charlotte down from Belgravia. It's raining and we are planning to spend the weekend in Hamble Marina. What boat shall I buy?'

'A Moonraker . . .'

Best powerboat story (2)
The late American racing powerboat designer/

builder, Don Aronow, is questioned by a leading American society magazine about his conscience whenever the US Coastguard catches one of his craft drug smuggling.

Reporter: 'Does it worry you that some of your craft end up in the hands of the underworld?'

'Yes.'

'How do you feel when one is caught?'

'Annoyed.'

'Why annoyed?'

'Because someone's building faster boats than me . . .'

Best powerboat story (3)

The scene is the annual Round the Island (Isle of Wight) race for offshore powerboats.

The very fast Class I (16 litre) outfit *Avenger* is leading. She has her owner/driver, co-driver, professional engineering/throttleman and HRH Prince Michael of Kent aboard as guest crew member.

Professional, West Country engineer to Prince Michael. He shouts in a broad accent above the roar of the huge craft travelling at 70 m.p.h.

'Hold tight, sir.'

The Prince is thrown against the cockpit side cutting his hand.

'I told you to hold tight, Sir. Look, you've cut yourself. At least I think you have, sir. They always told me it would be blue . . .'

Ocean Greats

Everyone with an affection for boats retains enormous admiration for the greats of the art – and if it makes the humble dinghy owner feel better, even the big boys must get wet sometimes.

Prince Philip, for example has been known to have the odd scrape off Cowes, once bumping into a guardship keeping sightseers at bay and on another occasion getting a ducking when another boat came too close to his Flying Fifteen *Coweslip* and she keeled over. That time, it was not all. On reaching shore the weight of the waterlogged boat then caused a crane to collapse and the Prince was almost decapitated by a flying 25ft main boom.

Edward Heath had the same problems of 'rubberneckers' coming too close, which once caused one of his four *Morning Cloud*s to strike the South Brambles buoy, one of the biggest in the Solent.

Falklands task force commander *Rear Admiral Sandy Woodward* had little trouble in the South Atlantic, but shortly afterwards was ignominiously towed into Chichester harbour by an RNVR vessel after his yacht was dismasted southeast of the Isle of Wight; though most ingloriously of all, former 'Yachtsman of the Year' *Eric Tarbaly*, who broke the record for the fastest single-handed Atlantic crossing, failed to make his way up the Lymington river in August 1981 in his 74ft *Euromarche*. He was left embarrassingly stuck in the mud for several hours and was forced to wait patiently until the tide came back in.

Favourite riposte by a world-beating mariner

Few will forget the first words of Robin Knox-Johnston, when challenged by a customs officer after becoming the first man to sail non-stop single-handed round the world.

'Where from?' asked the customs man at Falmouth harbour as he prepared to disembark for the first time in 312 days.

'Falmouth,' Robin laconically though altogether accurately replied.

Nearest Britain came to winning the America's Cup

The British 12-metre *Victory II* received an ecstatic tickertape welcome from tens of thousands of New Yorkers in February 1987, after the America's Cup was wrested back from Australia. What's that?

Yes, *Victory II*, tickertape welcome, thousands cheering.

It must be said that it was Dennis Conner who was with her, of course, and *Victory II*, well, she wasn't there for herself, you understand, but as a late stand in for the real victor, *Stars and Stripes*.

Realizing there was no 12-metre yacht available for the parade, New York had approached Peter de Savary for permission to use the British boat which featured in the 1982 challenge. Thus it was transported 400 miles from Newport, Rhode Island, to the festivities (a rather shorter distance than Fremantle, it must be said).

There was a rather tear-jerking quote from De Savary afterwards. He said: 'It's the closest *Victory II* ever came to winning the America's Cup.'

Jonathan Dimbleby

Well-known TV current affairs presenter

First sailing memory
It may not have been quite my first. It was a holiday on the Thames in my father's Dutch barge. We, the children, behaved dreadfully. I was nine. For the first time in my life I was beaten by my exasperated father with a hairbrush. But he held it the wrong way round, bristles against bottom. It didn't hurt.

Most embarrassing moment
Alongside at Dartmouth. In a rubber dinghy. Advising the children to get into the boat carefully. A large crowd watching. I am laden with bags and newspapers. I forget my own advice and step into fifteen feet of water and drop from sight. I surface, glasses intact on my nose and magazines under my arm to a storm of wisecracks from the gathering crowd ('You'd better stick to TV', etc.) and the children mockingly remind me of my lesson to them!

Biggest insomniac to win the 'auld mug'

No, I find it difficult to believe, too, but America's Cup winner Dennis Conner crushed the Australian challenge at Fremantle, in early 1987, after the most sleepless series of nights. While his teetotal Antipodean rival Iain Murray stayed off the grog and got his head down for some early nights, frisky Dennis was off doing his rounds of celebrity appearances, restaurants and bars. The routine went like this: after three hours of gruelling racing, and the sometimes just as gruelling post-race press conference, it was, in Mr Conner's book, time for fun. First: out on the town for dinner. Second: a cosy little bar. If he liked the bar, he would stay chatting to local fishermen and boat workers. Midnight: time for a game of poker. Four a.m.: time for a nightcap. His crew were concerned some of the time. No, not that he wasn't getting enough sleep, that he wasn't finding enough poker games. As an alternative, they kindly fixed it among themselves to set up 'tag teams' to talk sailing with the maestro through the small hours to keep him in the right trim for the next day's racing.

Newest and potentially most dangerous hazard to yachting

Yes, in the old days they didn't have it to contend with. But nowadays any great ocean sailor has to allow for it, put up with it, and invariably navigate around it. The name of this lethal and intrusive sea monster is television, and some famous names may rue the day it was launched on the air waves. Such as:

John Ridgway, who had to give up an attempt to race single-handed round the world in *English Rose IV* in 1968 because of bolts sheared off by collisions with two TV trawlers. This led to the mast whipping and by Recife in South America, Captain Ridgway knew he wouldn't make it round the Horn.

German helmsman *Rudi Magg*, bringing in his country's third and last boat *Rubin* in the 1985 Admiral's Cup. He was temporarily blinded by the TV arc lights and steered his boat onto a breakwater. Fortunately for him there were no penalty points. Unfortunately he broke his nose in the collision.

Finally *Peter Gilmour*, no, not the 'Onedin Line' version, but main-sheet trimmer on the Kookaburra in the 1987 America's Cup. He got fed up with the onboard camera which he was convinced was always spying on him in unguarded moments. Finally, venting his anger, he addressed the prying TV eye with a tirade of well-chosen words. He then asked whether it was listening. The camera nodded.

Most unexpected admission by a round-the-world sailor

Before Dame Naomi James set off on her historic round-the-world voyage in 1978 she had an unusually frank admission: she was a martyr to seasickness.

As she returned to Dartmouth a helicopter from RAF Culdrose lowered the record-breaking woman sailor a souvenir – the crest of his 771 Air-Sea Rescue Squadron with the message: 'Sorry it isn't mounted but time is not on our side.' It was wrapped in . . . a sick bag with another message: 'In case you need it.'

Replied an obviously cured Naomi: 'I was sick at the start but I am never sick now.'

Biggest sceptic on solo-circumnavigation

Sir Francis Chichester and Robin Knox-Johnston had their problems of course, but what, in the days without modern communication, or navigation, of the first recorded solo round-the-world yachtsman, Captain Joshua Slocum? He sailed in 1895 from Newport, Rhode Island, in his 35ft oyster boat *Spray*. On his 'way round' Captain Slocum found himself presented by a senior judge to the South African President, Paul Kruger. 'This is Captain Slocum who is sailing round the world,' nudged the judge. 'You mean *on* it,' replied the President, unmoved 'The world is flat.'

Earl of Dundonald

Noted yachting enthusiast

First boat memory
Aged six/seven I was driving my father's speedboat. He and about seven people were fishing for mackerel out the back of the boat. He asked me to increase the speed. The throttle was jammed. Suddenly the boat jumped from five knots to twenty-five, throwing everybody out the back. It took a six-year-old five minutes to collect them in freezing Scottish water!

Most amusing moment (1)
A friend went fishing with a business colleague who had recently purchased his yacht. They anchored at Dalgetty Bay in the Forth and had a picnic. As they ate, a swimmer swam out to them 400 yards and when he stopped alongside, the owner of the boat said he was a bit far out. The swimmer replied by standing up and only being chest high in water. Beware mud flats!

Most amusing moment (2)
A friend was driving back from Mull to Oban and awaited the Craigmuire ferry. A Force 6 was blowing with torrential rain lashing across the tarmac. There was no other car and nobody else in the area except the boatman huddled against a hut. He walked over to my friend and asked him: 'Are y fur Oban or Lochabie, sur?' 'Oban,' he replied. 'Then y're in the wrong queue.'

Three things that kept Sir Francis Chichester going

1. Fresh green salad, grown on his boat.
2. The vision of the first thing he wanted after 119 days alone at sea. 'The best dinner from one of the best chefs, in the best company I can have.'
3. The amber nectar. On disembarking: 'I think there is still a little left. I enjoyed the lovely golden liquid and I was terrified it would run out.'

Quietest welcome for a round-the-world voyager

When C. H. 'Rusty' Webb returned to Falmouth in 1968 two years and ten months after setting out on a single-handed marathon round the world, it was probably the quietest return on record. Among the interruptions to the fifty-five-year-old former Birmingham estate agent on his 35,000 mile voyage was being holed twenty-one times by a coral reef off Antigua (he patched the holes with canvas and copper sheeting held together with 1200 copper nails, raised the 9-ton sloop *Flyd* from the bottom, and carried on). To say his return was a silent one is the understatement of the book. Few knew until fellow members of the Royal Cornwall Yacht Club, of which he was a member, glanced across the harbour moorings and saw the *Flyd* tied up.

Brenda Dean

General secretary, SOGAT '82

First boating memory

Nothing, but nothing it seems sticks like Medway mud. Of course I did not know that the first time I went sailing . . .

I had more in mind a picture of idyllic peace, gin and tonic on the quarterdeck and clothing à la *Daily Express* Boat Show more than English east coast.

Our start was not exactly auspicious. My boyfriend explained there was something wrong with the engine which should have been enough to bring any sensible girl to her senses. But off we went sailing in a stiff breeze down river and certainly all went well initially.

It was only when we came back to our buoy that I realized how difficult it is to pick one up when the wind and tide are opposed, there is not much room and the engine will not start.

I think I got hold of the end of the pennant at the fourteenth attempt . . .

(Nowadays we do it the other way round. *He* picks up the pennant and I do the helming.)

As we made our way ashore in the dinghy I was still aware of the strong wind and surging tide. And in those days our club had pretty primitive methods of getting a dinghy on a trailer at the water's edge. As we struggled up the hard I suddenly lost my footing and fell flat (keel downwards) in the thick mud.

I distinctly remember thinking, 'Brenda, this is very definitely *not* for you.'

It seemed as if the entire club membership was gathered on the patio in front of the club house indulging in the spectator sport of watching a trade-union official at bay. And dripping in all directions.

I was so muddy there was no way I could go home in what I was wearing. Fortunately my boyfriend had a spare pair of trousers though they were about six sizes too big. As one who always tries to take pains over one's appearance it was very definitely not my day and the itch of the mud was unbearable. I couldn't get to a bath quick enough.

As for that Medway mud, well it may have something to do with centuries of the Royal Navy being at Chatham but it certainly is very strong, lethal stuff. There was no way I could get the trousers clean and they ended up in the dustbin.

We often laugh at my travails on my first day's sailing because it could so easily have put me off for life when messing about in boats really is a tremendous way of forgetting problems and pressures. I have often found time spent in a quiet deserted creek with nothing but a few kingfishers for company does wonders to sort out my thinking.

And watching the way those birds and the many other breeds so love the mud in the Medway and the adjoining Swale river is yet again a reminder to me that first acquaintances are not always right. Even if they do itch.

Sir Ranulph Fiennes

Famed round-the-world-explorer

Best sailing memory

When I was sixteen and romantic, my cousin, the fifty-eight-year-old Leslie Whiteside – who was rector of a church in Lombard Street – asked my elder sister Celia, my Scottish cousin Greville and me to go sailing on his 17ft boat. I cannot say whether it was a dinghy, yacht, knockabout or whatever, for I was then and still am, no sailing man.

Leslie, or 'Uncle God' as we all knew him, also asked along a beautiful eighteen-year-old brunette – another cousin, but a distant one – to whom I was at the time much attached (although she did not know it). Her inclusion in the expedition made me pluck up courage, for I hated the very thought of going to sea in a boat, and I accepted to join the crew.

The brunette was called Diana or Elizabeth and answered to either name. Uncle God used both at random. He was a vague and friendly sort but, as skipper, he tried to appear stern and commanding.

Two hours and one mile out from Bosham, our feet grey with clinging, odiferous mud, we escaped the gauntlet of little crafts and mudbanks and found the wind. A stiff one.

'Ready about. Lee O' shouted Leslie. The four of us ducked low and shot across to the other side of the boat, our weight transference coinciding with a lull in the wind and all but tipping us over. Our skipper was livid.

'Diana, you deal with the port sheets and you, Celia, the starboard.'

Over the next half-hour Uncle God consistently muddled the names Celia, Diana and Elizabeth when yelling out his orders to man the sheets. The result was total chaos, the boat shipped water and Gubby and I grew queasy. We slouched in the bilges feeling totally miserable. Uncle God bade us take over from the girls but, despite the gorgeous Diana's presence, all I could manage was a negative groan from the scuppers.

Nonetheless, for the following quarter of a century, when asked if I have sailed, I say yes. For I did, once, and that unforgettable experience has made me ensure that all my future expeditions in hot or cold climes steered well clear of small boats with sails.

Uncle God died contented on his seventy-eighth birthday whilst crossing the Channel in a sailing dinghy. It takes all types to man the world.

First single-handed row across the Pacific launched by a fall off a bar stool

London photographer Peter Bird found it hard to impress the journalist from *The Australian* one night in a New York bar. He was seeking sponsorship for the first single-handed row across the Pacific and was obviously getting nowhere. So he got drunk, fell off his stool, shouting just as he went down: 'I thought this was self-righting.'

However, the journalist being a journalist obviously was mightily impressed at this single-handed feat and, yes, *The Australian did* help Mr Bird buy the John Fairfax/Sylvia Cook boat *Britannia II* for his mammoth row, beginning with the plan 'I'll go under the Golden Gate Bridge at San Francisco and turn left.'

Regrettably *Britannia II* was wrecked off Hawaii but the false start was enough to launch Mr Bird on a second bid, albeit ending among matchwood on the Great Barrier Reef thirty-three miles short of the Australian coast. 'Please, please bring back assisted passages for poms,' quipped Mr Bird after being plucked to safety. No, he added, it hadn't been as easy as falling off a bar stool.

Largest number of comebacks from retirement

Met by the Prince of Wales, Princess Anne, and the Duke of Edinburgh after his 292-day 'uphill' single-handed trek round the oceans of the world, in May 1971, daredevil former paratrooper Chay Blyth vowed 'never again'. It was just the same story in

November 1984, when he was rescued off Cape Horn after hitting a massive storm while trying to set a new world clipper record from New York to San Francisco. 'Never again,' he said. 'It was the most terrifying experience of my life.'

A month later (predictably!) he was back at sea declaring: 'It'll take more than a capsize to keep Blyth from the water.'

In 1983 before the clipper record attempt he admitted to pressmen that he made the promise to give up before setting off on every major voyage 'as my wife Maureen knows only too well'.

One can fondly imagine the tensions between the two of them, and there is a story Chay likes to tell about his despair when his yacht *British Steel* also nearly 'bought it' off Cape Horn.

Remembering that Mrs Blyth had packed him a parcel 'to be used in emergency' he hurriedly opened it to see if it contained guidance, relevant prayers, or even a flask of Scotch.

'Imagine my feelings,' said Chay, 'when I discovered it contained a copy of *The Cruel Sea.*'

Most determined blast at defending his corner

The larger than life Uffa Fox, most outstanding yacht designer of his day, sailing guru to Prince Philip, Laird of Cowes, had a temper to match any bad weather out in the Solent. This came through, for example, in his opposition to the Channel Tunnel which he said was 'unthinkable' as it would 'damage the enthusiasm of youngsters interested in sailing'. My God, they'd be wanting to *drive* over to the Continent, he opined.

June Dixon, in her often hilarious biography *Uffa Fox* (Angus and Robertson, 1978) paints a marvellous picture of one of England's great eccentrics, a man who, rescued after becoming trapped head down in the water in a canoe, immediately did a full turn to impress his rescuers. He then berated them: 'I would have done that the first time if you hadn't bloody well interfered!'

My favourite stories come from his sometimes frenzied attempts to defend his boats or shoreline from occasional forays of outsiders – like the time he lay in wait for a short-cut cyclist (using *his* towpath dammit!) with a shotgun. He shot clean through the spokes of the astonished biker's front wheels then produced a dead rabbit from the seaward side of the towpath crying triumphantly 'Got him at last!'

Even this does not compete with the reply to a Royal Naval vessel charging up and down the River Medina on full speed trials as poor Uffa was engaged in delicate maintenance work on his 20-ton schooner *Black Rose.* After shouts from one of his apprentices failed to deter Her Majesty's Navy from going about its business Uffa grabbed his four bore and rained down a fusillade of shots in the direction of the naval vessel. It was out of range and fortunately no lives were lost.

On its next trip up river he was ready, loaded up and waiting. First he fired a warning shot across the ship's bows, then stood there pointing his shotgun at the bridge menacingly.

The Royal Navy knew that it was beaten and made a quiet retreat downstream.

Richard Giordano

Chairman and chief executive, the BOC Group

Best sailing story

The most boat crazy people I know are those remarkable men who have competed in the single-handed round-the-world race, the BOC Challenge. We have sponsored two of these races now, and a third is being planned. Many tales have emerged of these intrepid sailors helping each other at sea. Of course, being an international event, language sometimes hinders the best efforts.

The daily 'chat-show' is an important feature. It is a time set aside for competitors to talk to each other over the radio telephone, and often help each other with a variety of problems. On one occasion during the first race, American Francis Stokes was giving his fellow competitors a cookery class over the air, extolling the virtues of fresh-baked bread and explaining in mouth-watering detail, how it should be made. The Japanese competitor, Yuko Tada, whose grasp of the English language was modest, asked Francis to repeat the instructions for him '*very slowly*, pleece'. A tortuous half-hour later, having repeated many times all the instructions on how to prepare and bake the dough, Francis asked Yuko if he was clear about what had to be done. 'Yes,' said Yuko. 'But, Francis, pleece, wot ees flower?'

Best reason for risking your life circumnavigating the globe

I was much impressed by the words of renowned ocean voyager John Ridgway as he prepared for an exhausting 28,000-mile non-stop sail round the world in his 57ft ketch with crew member, Andrew Briggs.

'A chap,' he remarked, 'has got to have an interest.'

John Hannam

Conservative MP for Exeter, former Commodore, House of Commons Yacht Club

First sailing memory

I was a young boy of fourteen and was taken out on an inland lake near Farnborough. When we were right out in the middle of the lake the boat began to sink. There was much panic and we took to the water where some desperate swimming took place until I suddenly discovered the water was only three feet deep and the whole thing was a planned joke. My host had pulled out a plug and made the boat sink!

Favourite story

My most memorable cross-Channel race was in the early seventies when I crewed on Winston Churchill MP's *Contessa*. It was his first ocean race and there were three MP's on board – all representing marginal seats. On the return we left from France, and as darkness fell ran into a severe Force 10 gale and at one time did not seem to be making progress against the Owers lighthouse away on a lee shore. Suddenly the skipper in true Churchillian manner called on us all to sing and when no one responded his timeless voice boomed out 'A Life on an Ocean's Wave.' It was at that moment that real panic broke out amongst us and efforts were made – successfully – to get back on course.

Most bizarre experience

I became a fanatical '505' racing dinghy enthusiast, sailing from Lyme Regis in Dorset and in national and international championships. I was desperate for a win, and one lovely day with a steady Force 3 breeze my 505 took a huge lead and was heading for a great victory. Suddenly, to my horror, my crewman gave up all attempts to balance the boat on the trapeze and was scrabbling about around in the scuppers as my rivals sailed past. I screamed at him, 'What the hell is going on?' and he replied: 'I've lost my bloody contact lens.' We never found it!

Celebrity Salts

Celestial navigation apart, the sailing world has always had a close relationship with the stars. Some of it as a convenient haven for supertax earnings, of course: but from the Aga Khan to Tony Adams of 'Crossroads', many celebrities have found a natural affinity and natural extension of their aspirations by owning a boat.

Oh, and yes, I promise *not* to mention Richard Branson.

Cruellest welcome for a star of the Whitbread Round-The-World Race

This came in May 1986 at Gosport when a posse of ten customs men descended on Simon Le Bon's yacht

Drum, when a four-strong 'rummage squad' sifted through the crew's belongings for an hour and a half. Meanwhile the family, friends and fans of the pop singer were kept at a distance. The man overseeing *Drum's* equipment, shore manager Jackie Dodd-Noble, fumed: 'Just because Simon is a pop star, he seems to have been treated like a potential criminal.'

The claim that the raid was just a 'spot check' did not seem to be borne out by another raid – this time on *Drum*'s 20ft container sent by ship from Uruguay. This created even more bad news for the crew – dockers were left to repack the container and shortly afterwards, £10,000 of goods went missing, including leather jackets, personal stereos, cameras, tapes, boots and shoes.

Mr Le Bon said he wasn't bothered, however, and pointed amusedly instead to a cartoon in one of the papers showing a capsized *Drum* (in a position very similar to that after the Fastnet!) with a caption reading: 'No, the keel didn't come off – they were turned over by the drugs squad.'

Hammond Innes

Doyen of adventure writers, traveller and yachtsman

First sailing memory
Sitting paralysed at the helm, having gone about and straight into the Thurne bank.

Favourite anecdote
The sailing books we studied so concentrated on the problems of gybing that whenever we changed tack we invariably went at it arse-about-face. It was weeks before it dawned on us that, as long as we were going to windward (which was most of the time it seemed) there was a simpler way of doing it.

A dark and stormy night beating to windward in Force 6 and two drenched figures in the bows wrestling with the jib as they changed sail. 'You often come up 'ere mate?'

'Always glad to give a hand when the skipper's taking us the pretty way.'

Most bizarre moments
1. Greece and the mosquitoes so thick in the Levkas Canal we had to scrape them off the coach roof with a dustpan.
2. The man who saw a No. 9 bus off the Casquets and told the skipper his navigation was all to hell – the No. 9 bus, he said, didn't go where he was going.

Yachtswoman most reluctant to take a sailing holiday

This, you may be surprised to know, was 'Howard's Way' daredevil single-handed heartthrob Tracey Childs who told *Fitness* magazine in February 1987 that the last place she would spend her vacation would be on a boat. She explained that she had been filming in mid-Atlantic storms, thirteen hours at a time, but what really seemed to upset her were the sanitary arrangements:

'Half the time you're on a boat where the heads (toilets to landlubbers) don't work so you have to cross your legs for thirteen hours. It's fine for the guys because they can just go over the side as long as they know which way the wind's blowing, otherwise they're not popular. So there you are, crossing your legs with hardly any tea or coffee or anything to keep you warm and they bring along three riot control water cannons on a boat which pumps the water out from the sea in March. It was freezing.'

Tracey, who had never been to sea before landing the part of Lynne Howard and was given just two weekends sailing training, had had, she concluded, enough of water for the year and was looking to do 'a little gentle swimming in a hot sea'.

Worst sailing career for a head of state

President Tubman of Liberia had a regrettable sailing career for the man who headed the state with the most number of registered ships. (Albe them 'flags of convenience'.)

Under a Dutch captain, the presidential yacht *Liberian* three times hit the rocks in Cape Palmas harbour. Each time the President was on board. The captain was dismissed.

Under a Liberian skipper, the President fared no better. This time having sat aground on the rocks for ten days, his 742-ton luxury yacht then sank. Having decided his experiences had been somewhat inconvenient, he flagged that in future he'd go by car or plane.

Two reasons a famous politician took up sailing

1. *On his doctor's advice.* Premier Edward Heath told constituents at Bexley in September 1971 that his doctor had told him on taking on extra duties as Leader of the Opposition in 1965 that it would help him keep fit. Sailing, he said: 'Reduced my demand on pharmaceuticals. But we carry the necessary supply of pharmaceuticals on board at all times.' What pharmaceuticals were unspecified.

2. *To stop being bothered by golf club bores.* Until becoming a fully fledged sailor, Mr Heath had kept fit by playing golf. But, he told the *Sunday Express* in January 1987: 'I did not start sailing until I was fifty. But in 1965 I got bored with the constant questions about politics when I was playing golf and turned to sailing.' I suppose it's harder to push recalcitrants overboard while playing golf.

Worst puns directed at an ocean-going pop star

After the disastrous capsizing of Simon Le Bon's 77ft yacht *Drum* in the Fastnet race in 1985, the

Greg Barnes

Yachtsman and journalist

Favourite memory

We were delivering a 30ft sloop from Anzio to Corfu for the boat's owner. Suddenly a red flare blazed briefly in the night sky. Disbelief. Tired eyes can turn the flashing reflection of your own port light into a flare in that last, long hour before dawn. Ten minutes later, another red plume rose 30 degrees off the port bow – there was surely no doubt now. Ropes, harnesses, lifejackets and fenders were all made ready as we took bearings on the dying flare and altered course towards it. Another flare, this one dragged a strange tail of listless, incandescent sparks behind it – and suddenly the truth dawned. We had cooly and calmly been preparing to rescue a volcano.

We should have known, of course, that it was Stromboli – one of two active volcanoes in the Lipari Islands poking out of the Tyrrhenian Sea of Sicily. Even the pilot books say that jets of lava are often seen as ships pass by at night, but when you have done most of your sailing in the North Sea volcanoes do not come very high on your list of probabilities.

Reprinted from *Yachting Monthly*, March 1987, with the author's permission.

pop star had to endure some very cruel puns from the rest of the yachting fraternity before the start of the Whitbread Round-the-World Race just over a month later. According to Neil Cheston in *Drum* (Sidgwick and Jackson, 1986) these were:

1. Simon Le Bonkers
2. Durown Durown
3. You picked a fine time to leave me, Loose Keel (a play on the lyrics of a contemporary tune).

What made it worse, said Simon himself – who had written a song during the voyage – was that before the start 'someone had bet $4000 that I would drown!'

Two impressive acts of celebrity heroism

1. SDP leader *David Owen* won more than the usual plaudits in April 1985, when he helped to rescue five naval ratings trapped on a 150-foot cliff near his Plymouth constituency. Dr Owen spotted the youths while out sailing and acted immediately, racing back to the harbour and running to his cottage at Wembury to raise the alarm. A helicopter was called to the windswept cliff edge but conditions proved too fierce. So the gallant SDP leader held a rope as auxiliary coastguard Mr Peter Harris absailed down the cliff to bring each of the teenagers to safety.

Mr Harris said, 'These boys owe their lives to Dr Owen. Because of the high winds very few boats were out and no one could have seen or heard them from the top of the cliff.' Dr Owen agreed that if they had not been spotted in atrocious conditions, they could not have lasted the night. What did he say to them? Perhaps: 'You can talk to me. I'm a doctor.'

2. Comedian *Terry Thomas* saved three British tourists whose dinghy overturned in the Mediterranean. Honeymooning with his new wife, Belinda, he was in a pedal boat at the time when he saw the dinghy capsize and two men and a woman from West Wickham, Kent, thrown into the water. He said: 'We realized they were in difficulties, thrashing about and making no end of a splash. Belinda and I pedalled as fast as we could to the upturned boat. When we drew near we heard one of the men shout: 'Save my wife, she can't swim.' Terry Thomas and his wife jumped into the Med., then piled them into their boat and swam it back to harbour. What a carry-on, locals observed.

Most original yachting signal

I am indebted to Lewis Malandrone for pointing out the hazards of Commodore spotting – watching for the arrival of the Commodore to get his pennant to the masthead should he come aboard. Says he: 'This creates a scramble to find the missing pennant; it is always in a different pocket or missing completely. The other thing is to make sure it is not hoisted upside down. Guess who managed to get it halfway up the jack and had to do a quick double shuffle to get it right?'

That reminds me of Sir Thomas Lipton who was denied the chance for years to join the Royal Yacht Squadron presumably because of his over-zealous and over-publicized efforts to win the America's Cup.

This most colourful of yacht skippers who likened ocean racing to 'standing under a cold shower tearing up £10 notes' was, legend has it, so peeved by his continued blackballing he flew a very original pennant one day in full view of the hierarchy at Cowes. It bore the inscription: 'MOBYC.'

When asked at last by one of his erstwhile foes what signal he flew he gave the cheery retort: 'My Own Bloody Yacht Club, of course.'

Dame Naomi James

World-record-breaking single-handed yachtswoman

Best sailing memory

A story that springs to mind happened during a 'Super Sail' holiday. Groups of ten individuals or couples sailed with skipper (Rob James) and cook (me) on five-day trips across the Channel to France and back. There was an Irishman on board (honestly!) who was in my watch, with one other. In the early hours of the morning we relieved the off-going watch and I settled at the wheel to do the first stint of steering. Robert (the Irishman) stayed below for a while but then reappeared with two cups of coffee, one of which he gave to our second watch mate and the other he began to sip himself. Becoming aware of me in the gloom, sitting quietly at the stern, he gave a start and said uncertainly: 'Oh! Would you like some coffee?'

Closest shave for a member of the Royal Family

In August 1964, Princess Margaret had to be plucked from the Mediterranean by rescuers during a holiday with Lord Snowdon at the Aga Khan's new holiday development in Sardinia. Cruising around the island of Sofia, her host's yacht *Amaloun* hit a rock and showed all the signs of sinking. The Princess and her holiday companions leaped into the sea where they remained until picked up by

---

I hesitated, not wanting to show up his lack of good manners and replied carelessly: 'Oh, don't worry, just if you have some hot water left, I'll have some.'

He looked at me strangely for a moment but said nothing. Putting down his coffee mug he went slowly down the hatch. Not ten seconds later he returned and made his way carefully across the cockpit, holding a coffee mug. He had been so quick, it was on the tip of my tongue to ask 'Did you put milk and sugar in it?' but I didn't want to sound pushy.

He handed me the mug then, retrieving his own, sat gazing into the liquid darkness of the sea.

I took a tentative sip of my coffee, then another because I couldn't immediately understand what my senses were telling me. It was hot water.

I set the mug surreptitiously down on the seat beside me and wondered fleetingly if I was going mad.

---

local fishing smacks. Yes, she may have never met Roddy Llewellyn at all.

Loftiest put-down during Cowes Week

This can only be the salty-tongued positive battering of vituperation ('water, you bloody fool,' being the polite part) unleashed by an all-woman crew as the Flying Fifteen of a relative novice made for them on a collision course during a Cowes race in 1971. The helmsman wasn't used to being talked at like that, and seemed to lose interest in sailing almost from that moment. The man in the rogue boat was, of course, Prince Charles, and from that moment he seemed converted to windsurfboards and horses (cynics cruelly pointing out that at least he didn't fall off his Flying Fifteen).

Raymond Baxter

Leading BBC broadcaster

First boating memory
My parents took me rowing in a park. Was it the Serpentine? My father rowed at Oxford and took it all very seriously. I was perhaps four years old. At about eight, I went 'off the beach' in the Deal lifeboat and have been involved in the RNLI ever since. I remember 'Threading the Needles' in a fishing boat on holiday in the Isle of Wight at about ten years of age, and 'going down the slip' in the Sennen Cove lifeboat at about twelve. Since then I have never looked back, except with pleasure.

Least forgettable moments

I have called for help *in extremis* and, of course, the RNLI responded (Whitstable 1967). I have dropped the lock winch key into the water and dived to recover it (in the early Inland Waterways days, prior to my current boat *L'Orage*). (I have the best photo ever taken of *L'Orage* – at sea, in Deal Roads in 1980 on our return from Dunkirk. We are still wearing the Tricolour. It had been too rough to get out on the foredeck to take it down – *L'Orage* is a 30 ft-class Thames boat, not built for such goings on).

Best boat story

One which is typical of the spirit of the Association of Dunkirk Little Ships, of which I am the Hon. Admiral. We were crossing, in company, the troubled waters of the Medway Thames en route for Ramsgate. Year, perhaps 1975. One of our number was seen to fall back. Radio telephone revealed that he had 'an overheating problem'. Large pieces of boat were seen to be thrown overboard. He was actually on fire in a fairly big way. But the classic British understatement had survived the test of time and all was well.

Most at sea leader of a political party

Potential Prime Minister Dr David Owen looked anything but the nation's premier skipper when to mark the SDP's party conference in Torquay in 1985 he took out his gaff-rigged sloop *Milly* to pose for publicity shots. He had obviously been persuaded to carry far too much sail, and when the wind blew up, found himself unable to reef. He made instead for a cove near Plymouth where he blamed all on his boat's rudder. What made the incident particularly embarrassing for the image-conscious former Foreign Secretary, a well-known sailor in his spare time, was that all had been filmed by the BBC for a 'Panorama' special, which sure enough did not portray him as a man quite in control at the helm, or with his hand firmly on the tiller.

First Prime Minister the crew agreed to cast adrift in an open boat

While their skipper was Prime Minister, the crew of Edward Health's *Morning Cloud* once had a plan to cast him adrift on the briny in a rubber dinghy. Honest. Actually, this was not as bad as it sounded.

Indeed, the reasons behind the move, revealed in the book *Tack Now, Skipper*, by Mr Heath's sailing master, Owen Parker, and in his own sailing book, showed all the brinksman tactics of a Moscow summit. The plan arose because of the fears of the 'Sir Humphreys' back in Downing Street that an international crisis might develop just as Mr Heath

was out on the ocean, totally out of contact. Therefore his advisers came up with a plan for a sophisticated radio link which would allow a helicopter to be always standing by.

Hearing this, the crew rebelled, fearing all competitive edge would be lost by the weight of the extra communications gear required. Mr Parker said: 'To hell with that. We race to win and we don't stop for anybody, prime minister or no prime minister. If you want him we'll put him over the side in a rubber dinghy and you can come and fetch him.'

Fortunately for all, including Mr Heath, it was the last the crew heard of the idea.

Most boorish on board behaviour to a future queen

When on a tour of Canada during the early years of their marriage, Princess Elizabeth and Prince Philip suffered an extremely uneasy crossing to Vancouver Island. The worst moment of the trip came when a young naval officer brought them tea and cakes. As he entered the cabin, the boat lurched violently, sending the confectionery rocketing about the cabin. The officer was beaten to the retrieval by Prince Philip, but after picking up half the cakes the consort-to-be promptly sat down again. The officer gasped in astonishment as Prince Philip addressed the future queen: 'I've got mine. Yours are down there.'

Most inglorious suggestion for the naming of a boat

Lady Diana Cooper and her husband Duff (later Lord Norwich) were staying with their friends the Guinnesses aboard their new yacht, when the discussion turned to naming the vessel. '*Diana*' was one suggestion. '*Gloria*' after the host's wife, was another. '*Gloria Mundi*' mused one of the group. No, suggested Lady Diana, '*Sick Transit*' would be more like it.

One star sailor's worst moment

It is worth noting that the BBC switchboard was blocked with protests as a result. But in March 1987, round-the-world star voyager Simon Le Bon, questioned by a young fan, recalled his most embarrassing sailing moment as: 'Seeing the cook's **** at four o'clock in the morning.'

The Krankies

Famous husband-and-wife TV comedy and pantomime duo Ian and Janette Tough

Most memorable sail

We were in a summer show at Bournemouth a couple of years ago and took our boat with us, because it provides privacy for us to fish, relax or just sunbathe. One weekend Ian's mother came down for a visit and we decided to take her round the coast. Trouble is, before we'd gone too far the boat began to take in water. It couldn't have picked a more inappropriate spot. In fact, we had chosen a nudist beach! Poor old mum had to walk up the beach with her eyes covered and we tried to suppress giggles. We don't think she's been on a boat since that day.

(Fool?) Hardy Amateurs

The great and courageous examples of Chichester, Sir Alec Rose, Dame Naomi James – not to mention Drake, Cabot and Heyerdahl – have inspired some magnificent ocean voyages. They have also, to the chagrin of coastguards and rescue services everywhere, launched some great eccentrics on their travels, too.

[And, NB, we certainly do *not* mean the celebrities whose contributions punctuate this chapter!]

Shortest preparation for a single-handed ocean voyage

A forty-year-old Scots engineer from Fife turned up at a marina in Inverness one day in 1974 and bought a brand-new Bermuda-rigged sloop. He then picked up a map of Scandinavia, some food – and set off for a record-breaking voyage across the North Sea.

But the wife of the man dubbed 'the instant sailor' became worried and alerted the coastguard. His yacht was spotted one mile south of the Bass Rock heading east in gale conditions. Three hours later the police were told that he had run aground at East Lothian; in fact he had dropped anchor, given up, and rowed ashore.

Police persuaded him to wait for a favourable tide and do nothing more adventurous for the time being than sail back up the Forth to his wife and family.

Three pejorative nicknames no sailor would welcome

1. *The Ancient Mariners.* Best example: the two Scots, aged eighty-three and sixty-nine, who in February 1971 completed an epic Atlantic crossing from Greenock to the Bahamas in a 33ft sloop. The old men of the sea survived the seventy-day journey despite running out of food for the last six days of their voyage. Junior ancient mariner told how senior ancient mariner had caught a flying fish, salted it, and eaten it raw (at least it wasn't an albatross). The sixty-nine-year-old said he had been 'a little nervous' sailing through what locals described as an 'incredible' number of hostile reefs. The eighty-three-year-old who said he had undertaken the voyage 'to get away from the Scottish winters' said: 'I was too stupid to know what was happening.'

2. *Captain Pugwash.* Best example: the seventy-seven-year-old who, after selling his home to finance the trip, attempted in the summer of 1979 to sail from Emsworth, Hants, to Falmouth equipped only with a £5.99 radio and a lot of brass neck. He was said to have 1) misjudged the tides off the Dorset coast and ended up travelling backwards, 2) run out of fuel and drifted towards to rocky coastline, 3) burned a hand when he let off a smoke flare instead of a distress rocket and 4) been towed into harbour by a naval tender. He was twice rescued, once by

lifeboat. Finally, with his 23ft mastless, sail-less sloop run aground in Looe harbour he said: 'The journey was beautiful – one of the best I have made.' He said he had been criticized by coastguards 'only because I kept getting air in the fuel lines. That happened about six times – and also the rudder jammed.' He added: 'I'm not content to sail around the English coast anyway. Next time, I'm off to Spain.'

3. *Captain Catastrophe.* Best example: the thirty-year-old businessman from Wilmslow, Cheshire, who led coastguards a merry dance after sailing with two girls in a new 41ft yacht from Milford Haven. Within four hours he was lost. Coastguards then tried to guide him by sending all the positions of all the lighthouses on the southwest coast. The next day his engine packed up.

Captain Catastrophe, who said he was sailing to the Mediterranean, had then to be guided along the coast by flares put up by two different coastguard stations in a six-hour co-ordinated operation. He then had to be towed into St Ives by a fishing vessel; but there was another 'emergency' as the yacht was reported to be keeling over. It was found to be safely tied to its moorings. The boat next made it safely out of St Ives once again, only to send out another distress call shortly afterwards. The yacht was taken in tow by the Penlee lifeboat this time, while a coastguard officer travelled to the boat's temporary mooring at Newlyn, near Penzance, to give its owner what was described as some 'stern advice'. (Presumably starting with which was the stern and which was the bow.)

First 'Captain Calamity' officially beached by the Government

Former Merchant Navy bosun Bill Smith of Thuxton, Norfolk, found himself scuppered, up the River Orwell and without the proverbial paddle, in December 1980 when the Board of Trade slapped a banning order on his converted 75ft trawler *Doris* unless he improved safety measures.

Mr Smith caused chaos all along the east coast in 1978 with the most stunning of bravura voyages as he skippered his trawler (then called the *Excelsior*, the name being changed possibly to protect the innocent) from Fraserburgh in Scotland to a mooring on the Norfolk Broads.

Scenes of havoc occurred during the ten-day single-handed voyage when: He ran aground off Bridlington, Yorks., missing the harbour mouth by 400 yards and crashed into a jetty; he overshot his destination near Great Yarmouth by ninety miles, ending up at Ramsgate, Kent, where he ran aground again; and he was hauled off a sandbank by a lifeboat only to hit six other vessels, a fishing boat, a small coaster, an entrant in the Swedish tall ships race and a steam drifter converted into a floating museum; meanwhile he knocked several guard rails off an expensive trimaran and managed to get the ropes of a cargo vessel wrapped around his mast.

'It is normal practice to bump boats in a fishing

Sir Maurice Laing

Famous racing yachtsman, RYA president and former Admiral, RORC and Rear-Commodore, Royal Yacht Squadron

First racing memory

In the early 1950s I was in Johannesburg on business and, late in the afternoon, a friend asked me if I would join him in a yacht race in the Harterbrestpoort Dam, near Pretoria. I told him that I had never sailed – let alone raced – before, but he assured me it would all be very simple, that he would tell me exactly when to do and that, in any case, as I had been in the Air Force, I ought to know quite a lot about winds, the way to go, etc. I therefore succumbed.

When we got into the 12 sq.m. Sharpie, he explained it to me. I told him I thought a sheet was something that went on a bed, a cord was something you sang, a halyard was something you strung up a criminal with. This did not amuse him. When we got going he told me to pull that sheet, let go that halyard, etc. and, after about ten port,' reasoned Mr Smith. 'I plan to take the boat up to Norwich and then fit her out for a voyage to Australia.'

Mr Smith denied he had used an AA map to navigate, setting a parallel course to the M1. He said he had used a chart cut from a yachting magazine.

---

minutes, when we were well and truly last, he started shouting at me as I had not been shouted at since I was in the Air Force several years previously. As he was a customer, I restrained myself as best I could but was so incensed I promised myself that I would never race again – but I only kept that promise for five years!

Most bizarre moment

Just after the war we hired a pre-war 'clapped-out' Thames cruiser. Somehow I managed to put it well and truly aground stern to on the ebb side of one of the columns of a bridge at Abingdon. I asked my wife to push off with a boat hook and was horrified when I saw she had got beyond the horizontal. I shouted but was not quick enough to get the throttle off and she went flat into the Thames, watched by a hundred or more observers. It took quite a while to get her back on board – and that in itself was a lesson well learned.

Since then, with one exception, I have managed to avoid losing people overboard. Pity it had to be my wife who taught me such a valuable lesson under such humbling circumstances.

After being arrested and moved out of the way of the start of the Tall Ships Race, he was landed with a bill for £3000.

Reported the *Daily Mirror*: 'A sigh of relief swept the North Sea as news leaked out that his amazing voyage from Scotland to the South of England was over.'

Said the unrepentant – and yes, record-breaking skipper: 'I'm surprised by all the fuss. It was a pleasant voyage with no worries or hassles.'

Record number of rescues of a single yachtsman

Lone mariner Ron Davies, dubbed 'the scourge of the rescue services', set up an unusual first in August 1977 when he was towed to safety by a Cornish lifeboat. It was his seventh ocean rescue in a matter of months, having called upon the services of coastguards, lifeboats, helicopters and, on one occasion, the aircraft carrier *Hermes*.

Syd Little

Comedy TV star of 'Little and Large'

Most bizarre moment
We had a summer season in Scarborough and one day I went out with an organization called Fishing for the Disabled with whom I am connected. We had a great day's fishing, and on the return journey we started to chat. I noticed one gentleman who didn't appear to be disabled. I proceeded to ask him if he had a disability, whereupon he unscrewed his pot leg and threw it at me!

'The Navy lark has nothing on this guy,' said one coastguard, and the late David Penhaligon, MP for Truro, called it 'a longer running farce than the Brian Rix Whitehall comedies'.

The highlights of the life on the ocean wave for the forty-two-year-old Liverpool-born sailor who had left Belfast harbour two years before in his 'cluttered' 17ft Bermudan rigged sloop *Calcutta Princess* 'to escape the troubles' are listed below.

Rescue 1 came after he spent ten days trying to get to the Isle of Man. The lifeboat was called out and he was guided into harbour.

Rescue 2 involved another call out for the Isle of Man lifeboat when he got lost between Ramsey and Douglas.

Rescue 3 was similar when he set off for Fishguard but got lost and landed in Waterford, Ireland

Rescue 4 came off North Devon when he had to be 'talked into' Clovelly by coastguards. He had already been 'warned off' after sailing into the Aberforth rocket testing site during a live test of missiles.

In *rescue 5* his boat came within 20ft of being torn apart on rocks off Dinas Head after failing to make it to Milford Haven. A lifeboat and helicopter had been launched from *HMS Hermes* to save him.

In *rescue 6* he was found by the Padstow lifeboat off Trevose Head after becoming lost again.

In *rescue 7* he went missing off Land's End after putting to sea against local fishermen's advice and being unable to give his position by radio. He was towed back to safety again by the Padstow lifeboat.

Unsurprisingly, local feeling was rather against Mr Davies, but a benevolent Cornish garage owner offered him a Land-Rover to keep him on dry land while he looked for work.

He said: 'I think I can handle the boat well. I didn't ask to be rescued on the last occasion, it was the coastguard's fault for panicking.' As he set off by road one of the Padstow lifeboatmen said: 'I only hope the AA don't have to be called out.'

Two most venturesome trips in an ocean-going ferry

1. A lovesick Lancastrian could not stop thinking about Jeanette, the pretty French girl he had left behind after a day trip to Calais. So when he spotted an unattended ferry at Fleetwood, Lancs., in the summer of 1974, he decided to 'borrow' it to sail across the Channel to see her. Unfortunately, he

William Lucas

Well-known TV face

Three sailing home truths

1. I sail only dinghies or day boats now for one very good reason: ocean-going boats are manned almost entirely by world champion snorers. An orchestra tuning up has nothing on a deep sea crew two seconds after 'lights out'.
2. I have never been seasick. I have a theory about it: time and again I have found that people like myself who are never afflicted have another affliction in common. We all have no sense of direction on land.
3. Years ago while in the Royal Navy I was told by an old chief petty officer that seagulls were reincarnated chief petty officers. Having watched these birds over the years with their voracious appetities, inscrutable expressions, dogged determination and their ability to pounce at the last possible moment I have come to believe it!

---

wasn't up to the seamanship and fell asleep. He awoke to see Blackpool tower off the port bow. After admitting taking the £8500 ferry *Viking 66* without the owner's consent he was fined £50 by Fleetwood magistrates. He said he was looking for a job at Fleetwood docks to raise the money for a paid-for trip to Calais.

2. A seventeen-year-old Belgian teenager who complained he had 'nothing to do' appeared in court

at Liskeard, Cornwall in October 1986, after stealing a £15,000 passenger ferry and attempting to sail single-handed to America. The court heard he had just £7 in cash, a few pence in Belgian currency and only twenty hours of fuel. His lawyer said: 'He wanted to put some sparkle into his life. It was a story Walt Disney would have been proud of.'

The bored Belgian was picked up seven miles off the Lizard after a rescue operation involving the Royal Navy, police helicopters and a coastguard cutter with unsurprisingly not a Walt Disney fan among them.

Most optimistic trip to retrace Drake's footsteps

This was probably the epic trip launched by a forty-eight-year-old ex-Merchant Navy man who, in August 1986, sold up his camera equipment for £600 and bought an old boat, sail, and outboard motor, and set off to find a brave new world. Stocking up with a bucket of cheese, five litres of orange squash (you know how scurvy can get you) four bars of chocolate and large quantities of hand-rolling tobacco, our intrepid seafarer set sail from Newport, Gwent.

His sailing was far from plain. As he passed Cardiff his engine failed and he drifted helplessly up and down the coast with his unrigged mast lying on the deck of the 15ft sloop.

Worse was to come. He drifted in towards the shore, but this was no ordinary shore. It was a high-security Royal Navy torpedo range near Weston-super-Mare.

Lulu

International recording star and TV actress

Most memorable outing
During a trip to Vancouver one year I became friendly with a family of Canadians who thought we might be related because we had the same surname. Anyway, one day we decided to take out the motorboat and halfway to our destination it conked out.

One of the kids started fiddling with the engine to fix the boat, and I being my usual nosey self went over to see if he was doing it right.

I leant over to see what he was doing and he moved his arm, bringing his elbow up into my face, hard. I ended up with a huge black eye and had to spend the next two weeks of my visit, onstage and off, making up stories and jokes about the terrific shiner I had!

Our friend was arrested by a Navy high-speed inflatable whose crew called out the lifeboat. The lifeboatmen suspected him (spying all that hand-rolling tobacco – or was it the orange squash?) and called out the customs. He was arrested as a suspected smuggler.

A spokesman for the Swansea coastguard said: 'He was the original disaster waiting for something to happen.'

Norris McWhirter

Co-founder and publisher of The Guinness Book of Records

Favourite sailing anecdote

HMS *Battleship Warspite*, returning from the Normandy Beaches, June 1944 into Portsmouth harbour wearing the flag of a full admiral, found her way impeded by a tiny coal-fired drifter captained by a skipper RNR. The *Warspite* using a twenty-inch slatted searchlight signalled the drifter from a great height: 'From *Warspite* to HM *Drifter Ocean Wave.* Are you aware of the Rule of the Road?' Back came the reply from a weak yellow Aldis lamp. 'From *Ocean Wave* to *Warspite.* Yes, what did you want to know?'

Most amusing personal memory

From *Ross – Story of a Shared Life* (Churchill Press, 1977). At the end of the war my brother and I were both serving as first lieutenants in the Royal Navy, myself on *Scaravay*, Ross on *Shillay.* We were to be reunited in unusual circumstances after my convoy steamed up the Red Sea and through the Suez Canal.

At Port Said we received an extraordinary signal which read: 'To *Scaravay* from Flag Officer-in-Charge, Malta. On entering Grand Harbour, Valetta, berth alongside *Shillay.*' I worked out that Ross was now 137 miles away. At 3 p.m. on the afternoon of the 24 August we entered the Grand Harbour. I was searching for *Shillay* with my binoculars. I spotted her quite close to. Suddenly

I was conscious that both the pilot, whom we had picked up outside the harbour, and the captain, Lieutenant Commander Poynton, were in a perturbed state. The reversing gear on the main engine had failed and we could not reduce way by going astern which is the only maritime equivalent of applying the brakes.

A fast decision had to be made. Either we should have to ram the Egyptian Royal yacht *El Mahroussa* which was in our path, or to swing to starboard and strike the *Shillay*. The captain, with visions of diplomatic ruptures, courts martial and endless paperwork, quickly selected the wiser course. So accordingly, the unsuspecting *Shillay*, which was having a 'make and mend' after a prolonged spell of dam laying, was clouted so hard that she rocked under the impact. Her crew emerged on the upper deck, and seeing me, could not understand how their first lieutenant had got aboard the offending sister ship so quickly. They were totally flummoxed to find identical looking 'jimmys' in the two ships – an identity enhanced by the wearing of identical uniforms. Ross, who had not been expecting us for at least another two hours, emerged on the deck looking noticeably thinner in the face and rather strained – the legacy of his very prolonged hours under the cramped conditions in a minor war vessel.

Our collision turned out to be highly popular with the *Shillay* because it gave them four unscheduled days of shore leave while the dockyard 'mateys' worked to replace the buckled plates. The 'Collision and Grounding Report' exonerated us so there were no courts martial!

Biggest North Sea wardrobe mystery

It never got as much publicity as the *Mary Celeste*, but an air-sea search was launched after, in August 1980, a mystery boat made from a wardrobe was found in the North Sea. It contained a suitcase, briefcase, documents, packets of seeds, needles, razor blades, a primus stove – and the *pièce de résistance*, a pair of rubber gloves.

The 10ft long boat should not have been difficult to spot leaving harbour – it had a thin cotton sheet for a sail, and a pickaxe handle for a bowsprit. It was picked up drifting three miles from shore – with, chillingly, no other sign of the crew than those abandoned rubber gloves.

Four least successful record attempts

Fortunately little was heard about these improbable eccentric sailing firsts after their impending departure was announced to an incredulous yachting world:

The first man to cross the channel in a bubble. An artist from Llandew, Powys, declared in May 1983 plans to float across the channel in a 50ft plastic bubble. He would pilot the £1000 sphere, he said, sitting inside on a trapeze.

The first man to circumnavigate the world in a barrel. A forty-four-year-old adventurer I am pleased to report abandoned his world-record-breaking attempt after developing engine problems within three miles of his starting point at Putney in January 1984. The Port of London Authority wisely forbade him from going any further downstream without proper equipment.

The first man to cross the Atlantic in a converted water tank. Having twice failed to cross to America in a barrel a sixty-seven-year-old retired Glasgow building worker tried again in June 1985 in a converted water tank. Sadly (or not so) he got into difficulties and was towed back in by the Campbeltown lifeboat. He had trained for the event by sleeping in a converted chest of drawers, and admitted that his only real ocean trip previously was on a troopship in 1941 and that then he had been seasick.

The first man to cross the Atlantic drunk as a monkey. An ex-marine from Stockton-on-Tees announced his plans to set a new transatlantic record with four shipmates, all completely sloshed. He said (shurely with some difficult-hic), 'We'll take £1000 of drink with us for grog rations. Every other way of doing it has been tried. They've even been across backwards.' The Royal Navy declared: 'This sounds dangerous.' Yes, hic!

Most hopeful transatlantic voyager

A jobless nineteen-year-old decided to join the transatlantic elite by stealing the £20,000 aptly named yacht '*Stowaway*' from Cardiff docks. But he was rather hopeful about it, Cardiff stipendiary magistrate Sir Lincoln Hallinan was told in November 1983, having decided it would take him three days for his Blue Riband crossing (he believed the Atlantic was just 500 miles across) – and having stocked up with no more than three packets of biscuits and a tin of baked beans.

Fortunately for all concerned the would-be Chay Blyth's lack of navigational acumen led him to turning left instead of right once out in the Bristol channel and the stolen yacht was rescued after running aground on a sandbank. The magistrate put him on probation and he was told to go back to his parents in Nottingham, and 'get back on an even keel'.

The accused said he wouldn't be trying again. 'No, it's too bloody dangerous. Next time I will try and steal a plane.'

Most embarrassed lifeboatmen

In July 1983 the lifeboatmen of Harwich held their annual shindig with wives and girlfriends, in this case ninety of them enjoying a pleasure cruise on the River Stour. Sadly, their boat ran aground and they had to be rescued – you're guessed it – by the Harwich lifeboat.

Floating Capital

They may be dismissed by the purists as 'floating gin palaces' but can't we all take a tip from the megayachts in Cannes, Monte Carlo, the Bahamas and elsewhere sailed by the super-rich?

We may all hope, for example, for luck like that of New York restaurateur Gene Cavallero. In recognition of an excellent dinner, Stavros Niarchos presented him with a luxury yacht as a tip.

There was the wealthy US businessman who bought an exotic Persian carpet and couldn't quite place it in his luxury mansion. He ordered a £200,000 ocean palace to make the deep pile feel at home.

And then there was the Persian potentate who not only installed closed-circuit TV so he would view the coastline without having to budge from his luxuriously appointed state room, but also a spit for roasting whole sheep so he could make sure of his roast lamb and mint sauce.

Two most famous superyacht owners who didn't have quite everything

1. Greek shipping billionaire *Aristotle Onassis* had the *Christina* 330ft, 1770 tons of total opulence, converted for £1.3 million in 1954 from a Canadian

Philip Madoc

Stage and TV actor

Most humbling moment

Derek Scott, coxswain of the Mumbles Lifeboat, taught me something of the dangers of complacency one day when we were returning home after filming in the Bristol Channel for the television drama series 'Ennals Point', the story of a lifeboat crew.

As I played the fictitious coxswain I had spent some considerable time behind the wheel and grew to feel relaxed and confident. That is, until the moment when Derek, who was standing outside the wheelhouse, called me out and pointed to something in the depths and said in a calm, controlled – even good-humoured – voice: 'See those black things, Phil? They're rocks. If we hit them I'll have a lot of paper filling to do!'

With most unseemly haste I leapt back to the wheel and adjusted my course.

---

frigate. Named after his daughter, it boasted a crew of fifty. Here he entertained Winston Churchill, Greta Garbo, Maria Callas, the Kennedys – later marrying, of course, the widowed Mrs K., with a honeymoon on board.

Among the little 'home-from-home' touches: a Cretan mosaic dance floor which at the touch of a button descended to form a swimming pool, marble bathrooms with gold-plated taps and fittings, fireplaces of lapis lazulli, a staircase that was replica of that in the Palazzo Farnese in Rome, and a study decorated with gold swords and El Greco's 'Madonna with Angel' hanging over the desk. Oh yes, and the bar stools were upholstered with the foreskin of white whales: 'Madame, you are now sitting on the largest penis in the world.' What could you take aboard for the man with everything? Well, a cure for a hangover, perhaps. The *Christina*'s housekeeper used to say: 'I always forget the aspirins.'

2. International Arab 'Mr Fixit' *Adnan Khashoggi* ('Special 'K' to his friends) had of course, the *Nabila*, 282ft 1768 tons and worth £25 million. With a crew of forty, and named after his daughter, it was lent for the James Bond film *Never Say Never Again*. Guests flew in for cruise parties in his own fleet of jets – everyday superstars like Farrah Fawcett, Ryan O'Neal, Christopher Reeve and Sting.

Among the little home-from-home touches: onyx lavatories, dining tables in marble and gold, a theatre, disco, hairdressing salon, bowling alley, a helipad, and a hospital with its own laboratory. In the exotic state room tropical plants sprouted from a circular marble table embossed with gold. As well as a crew of forty-four, including sixteen cooks, the *Nabila* also boasted its own satellite TV link – at a cost of £10,000 an hour. Oh yes, and guests going aboard from his personal jetty in Marbella did have the benefit of a permanent red carpet.

All this could not have satisfied Mr Khashoggi, however, who before his little financial hiccups ordered a £50 million replacement with *two* helicopter pads, *two* satellite systems, anti-aircraft missiles, oh, and yes – what the *Nabila* was really missing, of course. *Its own submarine.*

Lewis Malandrone

Yachting enthusiast and writer

Favourite sailing memory

The story came to be known as 'How the Rescue Boat Was Rescued'. Having acquired a GRP cabin cruiser, I was delighted to be invited by Mounts Bay Sailing Club to act as a rescue boat during a week's racing. I am not sure whether it was me in whom the 'Mafia' were interested or the fact that the boat would do about thirty knots – useful when boats are turning over on every wing.

So to the first day and the practice race which will familiarize everyone with the procedures. Its eight AM control boats are moving out and together with mark boats, rescue boats are waiting to take up station. Referee buzzing around conspicuous by his presence, beach master and land-control base establishing vital contacts with incomparable efficiency.

Course layers have been trying to set the course in the face of the blustering wind which has been 'backing up' and changing bearing by as much as fifteen degrees every few minutes. It seems that the critical bearing from the windward mark will never be established.

At last the course has been laid and they are 'off', the sea rising and falling ten to fifteen feet, sometimes more – a courageous fleet of 150 small craft fighting its way to the windward mark.

Meanwhile, the auxiliary boats are spread out along their allotted wing watching and waiting.

All the radios are now silent. Then the boats start to arrive at the mark. It seems that they all (or nearly all) make it at the same time. What a scramble! Some gybe and others capsize – there are upturned boats all over the place.

The radio starts chirping and the rescue boats move in. Two boats have lost their rudder – definitely out. Fifteen have turned over. We pick our way through the swarm of boats and manage to reach the rudderless craft and attempt to take them in tow. Not as easy as it sounds with the sea doing its best to pitch us into their boats or them into ours.

A complication. One crew have made fast to the mast. Any attempt to tow would turn them over or pull the mast out. Using the loud hailer we try to persuade them to make fast to the forestay. Then we discover they can't speak English (how do you say 'Forestay, you Charlie' in sign language?) However we manage to get them both over to the comparative shelter of the mark boat. A euphoric sense of achievement prevails.

Then the radio again: '*Lorelie* – *Lorelie* – will you go over to the north wing? Two more craft in trouble.' 'Roger, Wilco – Out.' Away we go again, both throttles full ahead and the bows come up, for about fifty yards . . . then silence.

Horror upon horror. With all the pushing and pulling and chasing we have run out of fuel. 'Where are the spare cans?' 'What spare cans?'

'*Lorelie* to Control. Sorry, we've run out of petrol. We will cope. If the wind stays like this we will drift in.' *C. to L.*: 'Yes?' ▶

It is about two miles to the mooring and the wind should take us to a point from which a shore boat can take us into the harbour – in about two hours. Having drunk the coffee and eaten the sandwiches, we settle down for a long wait.

Into this picture of relative bliss a duty boat suddenly appears. They wave a rope at us. It is at least two inches thick and too big to pass through the fairleads, so we politely suggest we will be able to cope. The reply is succinct: 'OK, but you are sitting about four inches above a rock shelf. In about four minutes you will have a problem.' We quickly take the tow aboard and are taken to a safe mooring that could easily have taken the QE2. It nearly sinks us. We do not complain.

The shore is about half a mile away and we now wait here until all the competitors are checked in, the head count checked on the computer, the marks lifted and so on. Finally when all is 'lashed and stowed', a duty boat (it must have been the last one) comes over to us and with a very 'loud hailer' calls: 'We nearly forgot you out there. Would you like a tow in?'

Biggest megayacht white elephant

This was undoubtedly the *Shemara* owned by property millionaire Harry Hyams which, it was revealed in April 1987, had remained, crewed by a master and engineer, firmly in dock at Southampton for *fourteen years*.

Actually, the 212ft yacht, formerly owned by the Dockers (i.e., Lord and Lady D., not the T&GWU at Southampton) and purchased for a meagre £290,000 in 1968 had been out once – for sea trials in 1979. But it all evoked memories of Mr Hyams' Centre Point block in central London, empty for eighteen years.

The key was a dispute between Mr Hyams and ship repairers Vosper Thorneycroft after the yacht had gone into dock following damage on a Caribbean reef in 1972.

The dockers (i.e., the T&GWU, not Lord and Lady D.) said it all seemed sadly, a sign of the times.

Most novel use for a megayacht

Richard Burton and Elizabeth Taylor found an unusual way of making the best of their 249-ton yacht *Kalizma* when moored off Tower Bridge during their much publicized romance (this is where he gave her that famous 69.4 carat diamond). They discovered there was no better way of keeping their pets, thus avoiding strict British quarantine laws by keeping them off terra firma.

Worst put-down to a superstar who had spent millions

The perils of being a yacht owner. Peter Sellers' yacht berthed at Monte Carlo, was described by the *cognoscenti* as 'a cross between Sammy Davis Jnr's jam-packed mansion in Hollywood and some nineteenth-century Mississipi paddle boat'.

Biggest put-down to a superstar disembarkee

Errol Flynn once dropped anchor off the Carlton beach at Cannes. The girls on the beach screamed with delight as a boat was lowered and Flynn was rowed towards the shore by members of his crew, resplendent in jet-black uniforms. The scene resembled something out of the deep South of years gone by. One servant fanned the Hollywood star as he reclined in the deep plaid cushions. Another sang calypsos to his physical and romantic prowess, and his contribution to the US victory in Burma (he had beaten the Japanese single-handed, you will recall, without even leaving Hollywood). When he reached the beach, a smart elderly man approached wearing a black suit, collar and tie.

He promptly handed the Hollywood superstar a writ.

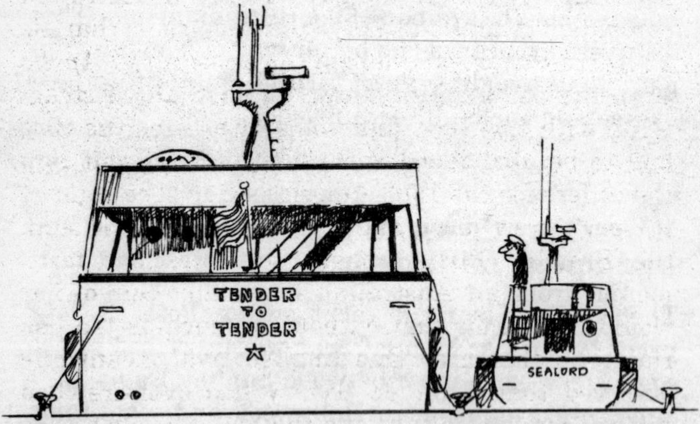

Tender was the sight

Japanese hotelier Frank Sakakibara was most pleased with his 5000-ton *Stella Polaris* – a superb yacht with graceful clipper bow, fan tail, and veteran stately lines, bigger than the Royal yacht. So much so that he ordered a sister ship. At 500 tons it would have been big enough for most millionaires – let alone boat enthusiasts – but it never had a passenger. He merely used it as a tender.

Biggest superyacht wagers

1. Dominican naval engineer and hotel owner Benitex Reixach, staying in Cannes, challenged Aristotle Onassis to a yacht race to Ajaccio in their lavish superyachts – both ex-Canadian frigates over 320ft – for a bet of £9000.

2. During Cowes week in 1981 England's America's Cup doyen Peter de Savary bet his Australian equivalent Alan Bond $10,000 in gold coins that his 12-metre *Victory* would beat the Antipodean *Apollo V* on the Solent. Sadly, after three hours of struggling with the most flukesome of breezes the race had to be abandoned with all bets being put into the coffers for the 1983 America's Cup. The sight of *Victory's* crew disentangling their spinnaker from the Bramble Buoy brought this prescient testimonial from an Australian crewman: 'Our owner would flog us for that without so much as ten bob riding on the race.' One English rival meanwhile observed that Peter de Savary had overstretched himself by wanting to take the helm. 'His job is to stay on the dock and keep the cheque book dry.'

Richard Mayne

Noted author and journalist

Favourite yachting story
My wife was dinghy sailing off Salcombe with two girlfriends, long before I knew her. She was crewing; a rather masterful girl was at the helm; the other friend, plumper and dreamier, was off duty. The wind was brisk, and as they beat upwind they were shipping quantities of water. The helmswoman was watching the bilges anxiously when a wind shift heeled the boat and brought still more water in. 'Bail out!' she yelled in a commanding voice. The other friend must have had RAF connections: she promptly leaped into the drink.

Wettest moments
1. The silliest occasion was on the last day of a summer holiday in the Lakes. We'd been to the Coniston show (sheep-shearing, wellie-throwing, etc.) and were sadly about to go home and start packing to leave. But my sister-in-law wanted to have a farewell sail in her Merlin Rocket. It was a cold day with a Force 4–5 wind, but I agreed to crew. We launched the boat by the landing-stage, surrounded then by wooden mooring piles. I sheeted in, and prepared to rocket across the lake.

No such luck. Whoops and splash – we were in the water, with the Merlin neatly on her side. Full of RYA enthusiasm, we performed our capsize drill: grabbing a sheet, standing on the centreboard, heaving the sail out of the water, rolling into the boat, emptying her with the plastic bucket on its lanyard. We felt brilliantly expert, but for two things. One: we were bang in front of the spectators. Two: we were in three feet of water. My sister-in-law had looped the mainsheet round a mooring pile.

2. Another private folly on Coniston Water. Sailing the family Wayfarer home with five children, one teenager, and two other parents aboard and about three inches of freeboard in a Force 4, I headed for the beach near the dinghy park, having slowed down by putting the boat in stays. Within feet of the shore the wind was suddenly flukey, so I asked the teenager (who'd never sailed before) to hop out into the shallows and hold us head-to-wind while we dropped the sails. He slipped overboard – and disappeared, all six foot of him. I'd forgotten that during the summer they'd dredged a channel for the old Gondola steamship, revived for the tourist trade. But it was a happy baptism. The victim is now a keen sailor and does it all the time . . .

Best superyacht plaque

Forget all that 'Love One Another' and 'Hold onto a Friend'. The best and most poignant message above the wheel on a megayacht was surely that aboard Francis Showering's *Silver Trident*. It proclaimed: 'A collision at sea can ruin your entire day.' How true, how very true!

Biggest bill for a quick tug off a sandbank

If you own a megayacht, of course, there are always those ready to charge you megaprices and this was the cruel fate of film and record magnate millionaire Robert Stigwood in September 1978 when the stern of his £400,000 yacht *Sarina* became lodged on a beach. A tug came to his assistance with, well, a quick tug. The local harbour authorities followed up with a bill for £40,000.

Most upstaged superyacht owner

When Adnan Khashoggi pulled his then new yacht *Nabila* into Monte Carlo in June 1982, he had a size problem. Well, the *Nabila* looked quite small next to the huge US aircraft carrier *Eisenhower*, and worse still, it was her crew that took over the entire town. Apart from minor inconveniences like the helicopter breaking down and the casino croupiers going on strike (this ended with a full scale riot with police and eight croupiers being taken to hospital) there was another put-down. An even larger white yacht skippered by Greek tycoon Stavros Niarchos then pulled into the harbour, and by this time poor Mr Khashoggi had had enough. He left for Nice, and quieter times, in an eight-seater Mercedes.

Unluckiest maiden voyage

The £3m superyacht *Brave Goose* was given a champagne send off from a boatyard at Teddington before making its way down the Thames en route to final fitting out (radar dome, etc.), and sea trials in the Med. Unfortunately the 350-ton yacht, boasting the latest and most sophisticated navigation equipment, fully fitted penthouse lounge, and dining room, two bathrooms to serve the master cabin and jacuzzi, didn't get far on its maiden voyage in January 1987. Instead it became firmly embedded in the mud after failing to squeeze under Richmond bridge.

National Car Parks chief Sir Donald Gosling had cooked up the idea of ordering the *Goose* (geddit !!!) from a British yard (patriotism dear boy) and the calculations had said that it would just make it under the bridge at low tide with a couple of inches to spare. Sir Donald said twenty-four hours later as he checked over his new boat at the Tower of London: 'We hadn't taken the extra water from all the melting snow into our calculations. We managed to get it through yesterday with exactly three inches to spare. You couldn't have stood a wine glass on it.' (Come to think of it, what's the point of owning such a luxury yacht if you can't stand a wine glass on it?)

A Thames Water Authority spokesman ungallantly observed: 'The *Goose* was rather a big one for that part of the river.'

Dame Alison Munro

Chairman of Chichester Health Authority, former senior civil servant and noted sailing enthusiast

How the sailing bug struck

I was put off sailing when I was about sixteen. Crewing for my brother seemed to comprise little more than getting very wet and being constantly shouted at to move my 'bottom'.

Twenty-five years later, watching my son and the same brother exulting in dinghy sailing on a family holiday, I became infected by the sailing bug and I thought I would like to 'have a go'.

Knowing vaguely how to 'go about' and which way to move the tiller, I decided to experiment on my own away from family derision. I set out when I thought no one was looking in my son's boat and soon found myself speeding towards rocks. I was struck by an awesome truth; to avoid the rocks by doing the only manoeuvre I knew meant turning back into shallow water or – horror of horrors – gybing.

I knew nothing of the latter art and the very word sent a chill into my heart. So, fearing to 'go about' and assuming that the water was very

Most impressive superstar megayacht disappearance

They say megayachts are *secure*, in terms of eavesdropping and the difficulties of assassinating those on board (James Bond, please note). But rarely can shallow, I jumped out holding fast to the main sheet. I was in about twenty feet of water and had to swim ignominiously back to the shore towing the dinghy behind me. I can see to this day my son and my brother who had witnessed the whole episode, rolling about on the grass bursting their sides with laughter.

I was past fifty when the bug got me again. I chose my holiday home near sheltered water (Chichester harbour), bought a second-hand Mirror and a book on *How to Sail*. I learned the first three chapters by heart and set out. It was only when I was well away from the shore that I realized there had been no guidance on how to stop! I sailed on towards East Head at frightening speed shouting at every boat in my path to keep clear. I finally crashed full tilt into the beach, but at least I stopped.

In the years that have followed and two capsizes later, I have improved a little and I am now commodore of the local club. But those early years have left their mark and I have never become the intrepid ocean-going racer I once fancied. But the bug has taken a firm hold lasting well into old age.

---

there have been a cat-and-mouse game with the press so much as the 1950s/60s romance of Aristotle Onassis and Maria Callas.

At times armed members of the Greek navy were called out to guard the secret of La Callas and her trysts aboard the 1700-ton megayacht *Christina*. Those on the jetty were ordered off 'on the harbour master's orders', skin divers and bathers were hauled out of the water by machine-gun wielding naval patrols: all to guard, it seems, one lady's dignity.

Peter Simple of the *Daily Telegraph* said: 'Was Miss Callas in Mr Onassis's yacht or not? One of the difficulties of this sort of question is that operatic divas seem to have got smaller lately and more difficult to conceal. In the good old days there was no doubt: the waterline disappeared, the decks were awash and great chunks of the diva bulged through the portholes. Some vocalists were so vast that they couldn't be got down the hatch at all. They were made fast to the deck, protected in port from prying eyes by gigantic tarpaulins.'

Biggest stores problem for a superyacht

Viscount Cowdray's heir Michael Pearson admitted in 1971 that he had a major problem with his £250,000, 125-ton, Camper and Nicholson yacht, *Hedonist*.

He had trouble finding enough clay pigeons to fuel the trap on the aft deck to try and keep his guests amused.

Best megayacht treasure hunt

This was launched by former singer and entertainer Madame Benitex-Reixach 'La Mome moineau' (the kid sparrow) who in the 1950s was most concerned to lose a lock of hair overboard in her husband's lavish 320ft yacht, the *Moineau* in the Mediterranean. She announced a $5 million reward for whoever retrieved it. (Sadly, no one did.)

Making Waves

Well, we all know how the sleekness of yachts, all that luffing and slamdunking, not to mention the fulsomeness of all those girls get the libido rising. And so it proved in the TV drama series 'Howard's Way' which in 1986 attracted the rather risqué alternative nomer of 'Howard's End Away' after well-publicized romances between some of its co-stars to follow up their bed-hopping on screen.

The *Sunday People* told how a perfectly innocent encounter between Sally Farmiloe, who played sexy barmaid Dawn, and Malcolm Jameison, who in the part of heartthrob fashion designer Clod (sorry, Claude) got taken the wrong way.

It was all about that thorny old problem – the locker room.

The couple were found apparently canoodling in the TV studio broom cupboard. But according to Sally: 'I had a collarbone injury from ski-ing and Malcolm said he would massage it for me.

'We started larking about and got worried someone might see us so he said: "Let's go in the broom cupboard." '

She added that she knew people liked to think the worst, but the props lady had burst in just after them and joined in the fun.

No, I cannot think for the life of me how that

nickname came about. But life afloat has always been about making waves . . .

Craziest scenes at the equator

There were high jinks on Simon Le Bon's yacht *Drum* as it crossed the equator during the Whitbread Round the World Race in 1985. It is a tradition, of course, to pay homage to the sea king Neptune and not for the high-spirited crew of this boat the quiet glass of wine or dignified singsongs of their race rivals. Respects were paid, according to crew member Neil Cheston in *Drum* (Sidgwick and Jackson, 1986) by the mixing up of a bucketful of filth and smothering of initiates from head to foot if they failed to answer an impossible general knowledge question. Said Simon: 'The boat was becalmed anyway. Magnus dressed up as Mr Pirate and Michael was King Neptune, disguised in crown and wool beard. We were expected to answer a series of silly questions. Whether we answered right or wrong, we were smeared with a mixture of fish guts, molasses and bran.'

Said Mr Cheston: 'Mike asked Simon for the number of people who live in Tokyo. Simon answered correctly, and breathed a sign of relief. His interrogator then asked for their names, and Simon's protests were cut short by a stream of noxious potion.'

Said the pop star: 'Never was I so glad to throw myself in the sea.'

Basil D'Oliveira

Noted sailing enthusiast and writer

Most memorable time afloat

We were anchored in Puerto Andraitx, Majorca, one night. The weather was good, no wind and a flat calm. It was hot. During the night, a very strong wind with considerable gusting came down from the mountains and the peace and quiet of the anchorage was shattered. Yachts dragged their anchors and the chains became entangled with each other. Crews came tumbling out from below to sort out the mess and secure boats and each boat put on its deck flood-lights. The whole process took about thirty minutes to sort out.

In the meantime the wind had dropped and it was again flat calm. We looked around and saw the crew on every boat – men, women and children – were all nude and not caring either.

Many friends were made that night, inhibitions

World's sexiest sailors

This accolade must surely go to one of the most unusual voyages: a three-and-a-half-month voyage from the Canary Islands to Mexico on board the aluminium 'love raft' *Acali* (Malayan for 'City on the Sea') with eleven 'swinging singles' sharing a cabin just 13ft by 12ft.

Six men and five women of mixed nationalities and religions, including a pollution expert from

---

were discarded and it set the pattern for the rest of the holiday with everyone sailing and swimming in the nude. This was quite different to the previous forty-eight hours!

Best boat story

I read this in the American-published *Journal of Marine Electronics* two years ago.

Heard on the VHF radio:

First voice: Our radar has you on a collision course with us. You should alter course 10 degrees south.

Second voice: We have you on our radar. Suggest you alter course 10 degrees north.

First voice: We have Admiral Goodman on board. Strongly suggest you bear 10 degrees south. This is a battleship.

Second voice: This is Seaman Farnsworth. Still suggest you bear 10 degrees north. This is a lighthouse!

Algeria and a French frogwoman lived on the raft while every action was recorded (well, I'll believe it if you will) as part of a 'research project' into sexuality.

As the eleven stepped ashore in Cozumel in Mexico in August 1973, to continue their 'activities' on a mock-up of the raft on shore, the leader of the project, anthropologist Dr Santiago Genoves said: 'We are still living in one room, still jealous of each other – and still exchanging partners.'

He went on: 'The trip was a scientific study of what normal men and women do about sex and general behaviour when confined together for a long time. Some formed immediate pair bonds and maintained them for the whole trip. Others just changed partners all the time. Yes, there were squabbles and bad feelings.' But, he added, 'there would have been no point if we had all been good little boys and girls'.

He declared: 'I don't think anyone got bored, but about half the crew couldn't wait to get off the raft and the others wanted to go on for three hundred days more.'

A raft was chosen deliberately as the most confined of locations so no one could walk out on the project – though one Briton jumped ship after his wife got upset on seeing photos of the girls on board just before the 'love raft' set sail.

The *Daily Mail* asked readers to nominate replacements and its switchboard was blocked by wives offering their husbands with comments like: 'He will be very handy aboard.'

One of those on board was a priest. Said Dr Genoves: 'He was just like the rest of us.' (He did *not* add '– insatiable.')

Most celibate sailors

The bronzed bodies of the superfit crewmen in the America's Cup naturally attracted the girls, and a new lithe breed of long-legged groupie named 'the cuppies' were identified flocking to Fremantle. It was sadly mostly to no avail, with syndicate managers insisting on strict rules to maintain fitness on pain of being thrown off the boat – in many cases, wives were also banned.

Ian Wooldridge in the *Daily Mail* reported that the exhausting race-day regimen – up at 6 a.m., bed at 9 p.m. – left 12-metre men 'with the lowest sex drive outside the Vatican'.

Eventually winner Dennis Conner was heard to greet one group of 'cuppies' on return to harbour with the taunt: 'You're safe tonight girls. We did 136 tacks today and they're bushed.'

First crew to cross the Channel just for a drink

Well, I assume they were the first. Steve Ackerman, twenty-six, and Derek Clarke, thirty-two, both from Bournemouth, launched an air-sea search in September 1978 when they went for a quick jaunt across the Channel in a tiny yacht with only the barest amount of juice (e.g., petrol).

They returned to Poole their dry throats having been quenched somewhat by a ducking after a near-collision with a tanker, the quick drink having led to a spell, well, in the drink.

Said Steve: 'We were in Poole harbour and it seemed like a good idea at the time to beat the

English licensing laws. The trip across took four hours, but we were almost run down, swamped, and I thought we were going to be drowned.'

Apparently the two spent several hours in a Cherbourg bar drinking Bourbon and wine, sleeping on the open boat before leaving again at 8 a.m. the next morning. Meanwhile helicopters were scrambled and ships alerted.

Coastguards said that no matter what anyone thought about the English licensing laws, the trip had been extremely 'rum'.

Wettest end to a houseboat party (or when they went 'nuts' in the Peter May)

The party had been really swinging on the houseboat on the river at Beeston, Notts, in May 1975 – until revellers got that sinking feeling when the weight of the festivities got too much and the boat sank ignominiously to the bottom of the River Trent.

The owner of the houseboat, the *Peter May*, Michael Reid, twenty-four, blamed a horde of uninvited guests for the abrupt scuppering of the event: 'Some fifteen gatecrashers got aboard. They packed together at the back of the boat. It just couldn't take the weight and the boards collapsed. Fortunately they all got off safely.'

Partygoers returned to the boat to salvage valuables before firemen lost a four-hour battle to bale out the boat and keep it afloat. The whole thing, they said, 'Just wasn't cricket.' The gatecrashers had been real 'stick in the muds'. Or in other words, a real load of 'soaks'.

John Ridgway

World-record-breaking transatlantic oarsman, now head of his own Scottish sail training school

First boat

In August 1960 I bought a 60ft 1898 schooner with three fellow Parachute subalterns. We sailed from Hamble to Cherbourg. All but two left at Cherbourg. Thence to Alderney in a predicted SW 10. The engines caught fire on entering harbour; in a gale I was awoken in early morning by a 90ft yacht impaling itself on our bows after it dragged out in the storm. I sold the yacht to a one-legged airborne hero who appeared on deck on the return passage by moonlight with stump uncovered. Result: violent sickness on ginger nut biscuits. I decided to take up rowing.

Geoff Pack

Former charter skipper, now yachting journalist

Best charter memory (1)
My most abiding memory is of our 40-ton ketch being caught in a squall in the West Indies. One of the passengers was nervous and disappeared below to spend his time at the 'heads'. Sadly the storm was such that he found himself being propelled from his throne across the cabin straight through a cupboard door on the other side. There was a terrible scream and I rushed below – all I could see was a large naked rear protruding outwards from the lower door. In a moment of genius the unfortunate victim suggested the best course was for his friend to come down and take a souvenir photo!

Best charter memory (2)
A good friend was skipper to a party of Texans who throughout the trip were thoroughly rude, discourteous, and unpleasant – they gave him a really hard time. At the end of a charter it is normal for the hirers to stand the crew a meal, but none was forthcoming. Nor was there any sign of a tip (ten per cent is normal).

On the final morning in Grenada they were off to the airport at 5 a.m. to catch their plane. The crew rose early and offered them breakfast – a very warming breakfast, they told them, of hot chocolate.

What they didn't tell them was that it was laxative chocolate and they spent hours speculating at their discomfort cramped on their small, 'head' less aircraft when skipper's revenge had begun to take its toll!

Best charter memory (3)
There was also the time when I skippered for a party of four – mother, father, twenty-five-year-old daughter, plus daughter's boyfriend. Mother and father were strict and the two lovebirds were allocated separate cabins. What happened of course was that as soon as mum's back was turned, our young buck would creep into daughter's bunk, creeping back later.

One night there was a surprise when mother appeared in prospective son-in-law's cabin demanding to know where he was.

'He's swimming,' I blustered. Fortunately he heard, scrambled out through a hatch and we all suddenly heard a desperate shout of 'anyone for a midnight dip'. This was followed by a loud splash as a naked form plunged off the side.

Few would go swimming in that part of the Caribbean, naked or not, of course, for fear of sharks, and I had a few anxious moments before the return of the naked apparition, ardour substantially cooled. Mother was apparently none the wiser for just what nautical exercise he had been up to.

Most confused racing skipper

Among many yacht race scenarios, I enjoyed the tale told by *Daily Mail* sketchwriter Colin Welch during the 1986 Tory Party conference about a friend of his crewing in a race at Keil for a chap who was rather too fond of the bottle.

'Amid much confusion they hesitantly approached and crossed the starting line,' wrote Mr Welch. 'The skipper, delighted, ordered sails to be lowered and champers all round. He thought they'd won.'

I am still trying to work out why this tale should say all about the Tory Party conference.

Spanking best frolics on an English river

An interesting alternative use for a Thames cruiser (and its crew) was revealed in a dramatic libel action in November 1974 brought by the owner who came to be known the length and breadth of the country as 'the spanking colonel' and 'the squire who went a-goosing'.

The People newspaper had accused the Colonel and former mayor of Chelsea, who had advertised for 'good-natured young ladies' to crew his yacht, of being 'a menace to young girls'. He was eventually awarded a halfpenny damages for defamation in a case which kept the nation on the edge of – er – its seat for several days.

A taped conservation between a girl reporter and the 'spanking squire' had revealed his requirements for girl members of his crew: 'A certain amount of jumping on and off boats, doing as you are told and getting whipped.'

He told how he had had a special cat o'nine tails made in the United States which left no marks, though in any case the girl could say she had slipped on a rope.

The Colonel opined: 'Every healthy normal vigorous male is a bottom slapper in mind if not in deed.'

The court was somewhat beaten down with a continuous steam of double entendres from the participants: 'Cheeky.' 'I'd bet by bottom dollar.' At one stage the judge intervened: 'Do you mean she had had her whack?'

Too broad of beam to be brought into court, the Colonel's cruiser *Adelaide Cottage III* was shortly afterwards reported laid up at Dunton's Shepperton boatyard – wait for it – 'having her bottom scraped'.

Most unusual ocean voyage

One of many strange vessels to be launched from the Antipodes was a 2-ton raft made from some 15,000 beer cans which left Darwin for Singapore in 1977 on one of the most surprising of pioneer voyages.

The two crew members said their aim was to sink two cans of the amber nectar every hour on the twelve-day 2000-mile journey, the 'empties' then to be sealed and fitted into special slots in the hull of the 24ft motor-powered craft, thus adding to its buoyancy.

No, and they didn't give an XXXX for what anyone else thought about their beer-can boat.

Brent Sadler

TV journalist, lately ITN's Middle East Correspondent

First sailing encounter
This was aboard a dinghy in Devon one summer: I knew nothing about the points of sailing, or anything else! As far as I knew there was a sharp end and a blunt end . . . a capsize was for canoeists I thought.

But in a Force 6 and what I later discovered was a gybe the tub went over, righted itself and then carried on sailing – me and a panicky novice hanging on for dear life. We sailed like this for over ten minutes before the inshore lifeguard rescued me. It was a brutal introduction to sailing but one I have never forgotten.

Most amusing boat journey
ITN assigned me to report on a man who was going to live on Rockall in the Atlantic. No expense was spared. Sadler and crew were taught how to climb so that we could go on the granite rock: ITN wanted hardened sailors to cope with the rigorous voyage.

The man going to live on the lump was Tom McClean, a well known if somewhat eccentric adventurer. The trip aboard a battered and smelly Scottish trawler was about three days there and back. The adventurer went ahead – we would meet him at Rockall. But unbeknown to us, bad weather turned back McClean's yacht and by the time the intrepid ITN crew arrived at Rockall our man was nowhere to be seen.

The trawler cost many thousands of pounds to charter. But not to miss out the ITN crew decided the boat and crew should fish to try and defray the cost. So for two days we trawled, and although it wasn't a prize catch the haul was enough to pay for a sizeable chunk of the charter. Luckily for us we didn't quite come back with ROCKALL!

Most curious case of a sailor left high and dry

Puzzled police were searching for a land-locked sailor in June 1980, after discovering a 17ft cabin cruiser marooned outside a pub . . . half a mile from the nearest water.

The pleasure craft *The Sting* was not only something of a tourist sight outside the pub at Taplow, Bucks, but a traffic hazard, too, marooned bang in the middle of the busy A4 and causing chaos to traffic.

'It's a complete mystery how it got there and who it belongs to,' said a police spokesman. 'We don't know if it has fallen off the back of a lorry or whether the owners left it there and forgot about it.'

The boat was marked down officially as 'lost property'.

Freshwater Interlude

This book could hardly be complete without a look at our Inland Waterways, which covers in fact boating lives as disparate (no, I didn't say desperate) as crewing at Henley or spending a life squeezed between the planks of a West Midlands narrowboat.

What binds these different worlds together, of course, is not just the tranquillity and caps but nostalgia for the past: either for the sunny unhurried university days of yore or the heat of the Victorian industrial revolution. It's J. K. Jerome to real ale (plus probably more sewage outfalls than the open sea). But make no mistake of the popularity of river and canal cruising: the Inland Waterways Association has grown from six to 20,000 members in forty years, and last year some 300,000 people took to canal and broad for their holidays. And how can you get seasick?

How three men in a boat became all at sea in a railway tunnel

'The sort of caper Compo, Clegg and Seymour would get up to,' wrote the *Daily Express's* Derek Hornby, and it did happen in 'Last of the Summer Wine' country.

'There was even someone named Batty involved,'

he added, 'though any resemblance to wrinkle-stockinged Nora was purely coincidental.'

What happened one fateful day in January 1987 was that three men in a rubber dinghy became stranded after it burst as they were trying to explore a three-mile-long disused canal tunnel near Holmfirth, West Yorks – Britain's longest.

The daredevil threesome managed to scramble to safety on a tiny ledge of rubble before huddling together for safety in the dark. One of the trio finally waded out for help the following morning.

It was not the end of their trouble. British Rail told them they would sue for trespass.

Biggest canal press gang

It was described as 'like a scene from one of the old Ealing comedies' in September 1971, as sixty-four landlubbers were press-ganged into hopping aboard a canal barge at Kennington, Oxfordshire, after the boat became wedged under a bridge.

The skipper reckoned that the extra weight would lower the boat in the water and get him free. The extra weight did lower the boat in the water all right – so much so that it sprang a leak and began to sink.

The order was then given to the sixty-four: 'Abandon ship' and there was mayhem as they simultaneously scrambled for the bank. The boat, meanwhile suddenly becoming much lighter, sprung upwards and became even more firmly stuck.

Finally the barge was freed using ballast instead of live weight. It limped back to the bank listing heavily, still leaking, minus rudder and with its funnel knocked off.

First-ever yacht sunk by a car

Yachtsman Barry Norris couldn't believe it. One minute he was happily sailing his £10,000 cruiser along a quiet stretch of the Leeds-Liverpool canal. The next he was suffering a slipped disc as he fought to rescue his possessions as his 25ft boat keeled over and went down.

No other boats were involved in the accident in April 1981 and there was no navigational error. Sadly, Mr Norris had collided with a sports car which had been stolen three days earlier and dumped in the canal. The submerged vehicle ripped a massive hole in the hull, water poured in and turned it over.

Mrs Norris said: 'Luckily we managed to scramble to safety, but my husband injured himself lifting items out of the yacht.'

Most unusual request after a canal rescue

Marco Hendriks, six, and brother Jaco, four, had their own Poseidon adventure when their father's 87-ton barge *Jo* capsized on the Mitterrand Canal in West Germany in February 1972. Mr Hendriks and his wife swam to safety, but it was thought the boys had drowned. But as the upturned boat was brought to the bank they were heard tapping and cut free from an air pocket in the hulk with oxy-acetylene equipment. The boys' first words on being freed: 'Daddy, take us on another trip soon.'

Most incredible canal by-law

Boatman Martin Toms lost a contract in July 1982 to ferry day trippers in his horse-drawn barge to Bosworth Battlefield, Leicestershire. The reason: a British Waterways decree that towpaths should *not* be used for towing. Visitors subsequently travelled by motor boat.

Six compelling reasons for canal-going

I am indebted to my former colleague Robin Stringer for an article in the *Daily Telegraph* in August 1986 which revealed these persuasive attractions of being afloat on Britain's Inland Waterways.

1. You could see kingfishers every day (though perhaps not on the Aire and Calder Navigation).

2. Birmingham has more miles of canals than Venice. You could spend two days going round England's second capital and half the time not realize you're in the city. (I won't say thank goodness.)
3. You can make interesting new friends. Witness this ad in the National Waterways Festival magazine: 'Small friendly narrow boat, non-smoker, new waterpump and fairly new fenders, wishes to meet similar with view to midnight

John Carter

Leading travel writer, presenter of BBC TV's 'Holiday' series

Best inland waterways memory
I remember filming a story about horse-drawn canal boats somewhere in England, several years ago. The film was very lyrical, as we were lucky with the weather. Unfortunately the horse dropped dead on the second day, and its replacement looked so unlike it that we had much trouble cutting the whole film together.

Best cruise ship memory
The Union Castle ships were great. Or rather, the staff were wonderful characters. There was an Irish ship's doctor who convinced me that the camel

rendezvous behind the boatshed. Apply Box 3616 and ask for Twiglet.'

4. Peace of mind.
5. Introducing other people to a world which has given you so much pleasure.

But, arguably most important of all:

6. You can't be charged with being drunk in charge of a narrow boat.

---

was the only quadruped that could not swim – its centre of gravity being so high – and caused me to print that fact in *The Times*.

The stewards were gems. If they disapproved of any item in one's formal wardrobe it would be replaced by something better from the ship's shop. I was often told that as 'our' dress socks were dingy and 'we' had taken the liberty of buying 'us' a new pair.

One day, on *Windsor Castle*, I returned to my cabin after watching the ship's officers playing the passengers at cricket on a suitably netted part of the deck. My steward was tinkering with my dinner suit and asked if I had seen a school of dolphins that had been following the ship for part of the afternoon. 'I didn't notice them as I was watching the cricket match,' I said. 'Ah, you wouldn't have seen them, sir,' he replied. 'They were well past square leg.'

The boating family who became high and dry after someone pulled the plug

No one could have believed it when a Danish family became castaways in the heart of England after someone literally pulled the plug and their canal vanished.

It was a mile-long stretch of the Chesterfield and Stockwith Canal at Retford, Notts, in fact, which disappeared with a mighty gurgle in August 1973 when workmen accidentally disturbed a giant iron chain attached to a 200-year-old plug which everyone had forgotten was there.

Millions of gallons of water emptied from the canal into the River Idle as if it were draining from a bathtub when workmen on dredging operations accidentally pulled the chain. They failed to realize what they had done and happily whistled off for a tea break. When they returned there was no water in the formerly 10ft deep canal – only irate boatowners and two dozen craft, including the Severn Trent Water Authority dredger, left high and dry.

Police sent to investigate 'a whirlpool' had to help the Danish family who reported that for obvious reasons, i.e., lack of water, they were unable to return their boat to the hirers at West Stockwith. The police plugged the gap by ferrying their car to Retford.

Only lock gates at each end of the mile-long 'dry' stretch prevented the whole canal from going down the drain.

British Waterways helped out with a new plug and eventually managed to refill the canal. A spokesman said: 'The little mishap had one good result. There has been a history of leakage on this section for years which we could not understand. Now at least we know where the water has been going.'

First former Prime Minister to get a ducking

Former First Lord of the Treasury Mr James Callaghan fell 'sweetly' into the river and had to be rescued in July 1987 after an extravagant charity bathe-in organized by former boat race cox and Olympic rowing medallist Colin Moynihan MP.

'Sunny Jim' was one of a number of famous political names who toppled into the murky waters of Old Father Thames while taking part in a nautical donkey derby to raise £20,000 for St Margaret's Church, Westminister.

Other sights included the former solicitor general, Sir Ian Percival, windsurfing down the Thames, an all-female eight dubbed 'the Avon ladies' carrying all before them, Mr Geoffrey Dickens, heaviest competitor at twenty-one stone rowing for all he was worth, and the Archbishop of Canterbury, Dr Runcie looking on in enchanted bemusement.

Fortunately, after the accident to Mr Callaghan's boat, a St John's Ambulance launch bore down swiftly on the ex-Prime Ministerial party and dragged bedraggled Labour MPs 'kicking and spitting' on board, according to one watching scribe.

Tory MPs taking part had meanwhile been told by their Whips in case of disaster to shout out their majorities, so they could be rescued in order of merit in case of sodden (sorry, sudden) by-elections.

Leif Mills

General Secretary, Banking, Insurance, and Finance Union and long-term rowing enthusiast

Favourite rowing memory

The Boston Marathon is the longest rowing race in the country. The course is from Lincoln to Boston and is some thirty-one miles. (It is variously referred to, including 'The Oarsmen's Armageddon'.)

I was stroking a coxed four and, of course, at the start there is a great deal of excitement on seeing all the crews start in what is a very long race. Unfortunately, our happy send-off was marred by the fact that our boat was violently jerking from side to side and I discovered after a while that it was all my fault because my oar had been put in the gate on the wrong side of the rigger.

Most showstopping entrance at Henley

This accolade must surely go to the drunken thirty-year-old Dublin-born hairdresser who in the summer of 1978 managed single-handedly to scupper one of Henley's most prestigious races before slithering into the drink clutching a glass of champagne.

Later a court at Maidenhead heard how the mad crimper's one-over-the-eight antics so incensed the crowd he had to be escorted to a nearby boathouse for his own safety. There he told a Thames navi-

---

This somewhat spoilt the start, but we did finish the course and the object of the marathon is to finish (crews finishing get a T-shirt or pennant).

The course is mainly made up of artificial canals (partly the River Witham), cut into the land with high banks. As there is only one lock and hardly any landmarks it is difficult to tell how far you have gone. It is as much a psychological challenge as a race.

I recall shouting to a woman on the bank when I thought we were nearly home how many miles we had to go. The innocent lady on the bank shouted back: 'Five miles.'

I was sure she was deliberately making fun of us and so subjected her to a choice of language which I had last used during my service in the army.

Sadly, painfully, and embarrassingly for me as it turned out, she was absolutely right.

---

gation inspector: 'I can hear you now – there are no waves in this cabin.'

The court heard that the half-cut hair stylist, who was fined £80 with £50 costs, had managed to saunter onto the course backwards in his motorized dinghy just as Leander and London Rowing Club were lined up for the important Challenge Cup race.

Despite choice expletives from the bank, he managed to steer a course straight for Leander, straight into the oar of the eight's No. 2.

The Irishman could not remember what had happened, he said. 'Suddenly there were all these official boats and me and the crowd roaring for my blood. I certainly don't recall falling into the water and holding a champagne glass aloft. I suppose they thought I was a bounder and a cad.'

Poor old Leander must have been motivated afterwards to give their foe the unkindest cut of all. They were ahead when he hit them amidships. The race was called off and they lost the re-run.

Best boat race 'own goal'

It is difficult whether this should be laid at the door of the Cambridge cox, Peter Hobson, who before the start of the 1984 race managed to slam the £7000 light blues boat into a stationary barge, thus causing it to break in two; or the BBC, who having spent a fortune to bring the same event to millions, (including flying a helicopter overhead) managed to miss the decisive moment of impact.

After the non-race it was revealed, with supreme irony, that it was not Mr Hobson's first encounter with a large moored object. Supremely tempting fate, he had listed his hobby in the boat race programme as 'reshaping barges'.

Most amazing result in a boat race

This can only be the 'dead heat' pronounced in 1877 when everyone had assumed that Oxford had won, but the finishing judge's declaration (he was 'retired' afterwards) was somewhat different. He was known as 'honest' John Phelps and in the popular idiom his proclamation became 'Dead heat to Oxford, by five feet'.

Despite most of the newspapers declaring for the dark blues, 'honest John' could not be found in the confusion of boats after the race. Oxford had been well ahead but near the finish their bow man hit a wave and his blade broke almost clean off; so they effectively struggled to finish with seven men.

When 'honest John' reported to the umpire, his decision was accepted as final. He was described as 'well over seventy, and had been so for several years . . . he was a bit blind.'

Oxford were left with the humiliation of doing a victory parade in their launch only later to be informed of the dreadful truth. Poles were hereafter erected at Mortlake to assist the judge and avoid the gentleman's equivalent of the claim: 'We wuz robbed.'

Most unusual race ambition

This was listed by Oxford reserve cox Louise Ainsworth, aged twenty, of New College, in 1987, and I record her words without comment: 'To satisfy the Oxford University Boating Club and all the college captains at the same time.' The mind does boggle rather.

Sir Leslie Young

Chairman, British Waterways Board

Most amusing outing

During the first week I was chairman of the British Waterways Board, my wife and I decided to have a week on the canals and our travels took us to the Foxton Flight. We were moored at the top flight in early evening, waiting for the locks to be opened the following morning so that we could travel to Market Harborough. There were a number of boats around, including one which seemed to be full of young executives in their twenties, obviously having a very good time.

The following day we went down Foxton Flight to Market Harborough and we returned that same evening to the top of the flight. The boat with the young people on moored next to ours and in chatting one of them said to me: 'I don't know whether you know it, but the new chairman of the British Waterways Board went down the Foxton Flight ahead of us this morning to a champagne lunch and reception at Market Harborough.'

I was in two minds as to what I should say, but decided to admit that I was in fact the new chairman of BWB, but alas there had been neither reception nor any champagne!

Boat Crazy

After escaping drowning, suffocation and being blown to bits when their trimaran capsized and leaked propane gas into their cabin in May 1979, a boat-wrecked couple staggered dishevelled seven miles along a New Zealand beach to the nearest coastal hamlet.

Then their trouble really began. They were mistaken for burglars and turned away.

'Peterborough' in the *Daily Telegraph* in April 1986 told of the Falmouth yacht chandler who sold a pair of boat shoes to an Irish visitor. In the heels were insets, red for port and green for starboard. An hour later the customer reappeared, demanding a refund on the grounds the pair didn't match.

Yes, some people are just *boat crazy*.

Des Sleightholme

Doyen of yachting writers, former editor Yachting Monthly

Best true story

We lived in a lonely cottage in the woods by the seashore several miles from the nearest lonely cottage, a place rarely reached by strangers. My father was fanatical about quietude and he dearly liked his sleep, even nightingales constituted a major noise hazard. When my sister bought the puppy it was evident that on its first night at least there would be doggy noises.

'What the hell can we do?' she asked me. 'The boat,' I said with sudden inspiration. Down on the beach, out of sight from the cottage, behind dense thicket was the cabin cruiser – a financial disaster of mine representing fifty quid, sans engine but plus a great gash in its steel bottom where my scraper had gone straight through.

'Won't he hear it though?'

'I doubt it. Tell you what, why don't I go down and lock myself in and make a few dog noises while you listen?' She liked the idea.

It was dusk, utterly still, remote, not another living soul about. I went down to the boat, climbed aboard, locked myself into the tiny cabin and sat down. I cleared my throat. Now I don't know about you but wolf howls, short agonized barks and whimpers are not in my usual repertoire and it took a while to get going. Then I got the hang of it. I sat with my chin high, eyes closed, lips pursed and sent howl after howl echoing and batting around the cabin. I began to enjoy it. 'Wowoooowoo' I howled. 'Wooooooow.'

On the opposite side of the cabin and facing me there were two small portholes. I opened my eyes. At each porthole there was a face, two goggle-eyed horrified faces staring in dread fascination. My howl ended abruptly. 'Ah,' I said. 'Evening.'

But they had gone. I scrambled out of the cabin to see two figures legging it across the shingle.

'Hey,' I yelled. 'I can explain . . .'

It happened all of forty years ago. It is a disturbing thought that somewhere on the Isle of Wight there must be two old men who will tell a strange tale, if pressed hard enough, of a ghastly experience, of werewolves and bared, bloody fangs.

First motorist to take his car water ski-ing

They didn't have a speedboat, but the two friends did have a wet suit, skis and a Volvo estate. So they had a brainwave. Why didn't they use *the car* for a spot of water ski-ing.

Well, water ski-ing became water sinking for the pair of pioneers at Barrow-on-Trent, Derbyshire, in May 1987. At first, sure enough, the skier rose statuesquely in the water as the friend towed him by car along the River Trent towpath. But as astonished dinghy owners looked on, the car driver lost control and his vehicle plunged well and truly into the murky depths.

'A shame really,' said a police spokesman. 'By all accounts, up to then, they were doing quite well.'

Most unusual hazard call to yachts in the English Channel

It was definitely not a British Telecom announcement when Devon coastguards in 1982 reported an unusual menace to yachts ten miles off the Devon coast – a forest of telegraph poles forming something of an unnatural barrier from Plymouth to Torbay. Perhaps not surprisingly, no calls were received reporting them missing.

Best yachting magazine hoax

This came in 1970 when the now defunct magazine *Yachting and Boating* published a spellbinding article in its London Boat Show issue on a new menance to boat owners called the 'polyestermite' or super-gribble. This ravenous crustacean allegedly devoured the hulls of glassfibre boats with both alacrity and pirana-like ferocity.

The author Bill Beavis told in *Off Watch. A Selection of Bunkside Reading* (Granada, 1979) how the spoof took off, with even the Natural History Museum ringing up. 'By summer the enquiries had gone international and polyestermites were responsible for a harbour buoy disappearing in Durban, for ruining one country's Admiral Cup chances, and even disrupting the oil flow at a Gulf port,' he wrote.

The sinister creatures, which in their 'frenzy' during the mating season were capable of munching through four times their own weight, were said to have been first found eating plastic detergent bottles in the Hudson River, which had made them a firm friend of the Friends of the Earth and led to their being adopted as a motif by a Winsconsin enviromentalist running for Congress. Their worst feature was, however, the possession of a mouth at both ends which meant the little blighters could 'lie back on a marina and eat two boats at once'.

Mr Beavis reported that thankfully, at least one person had seen the joke after a wooden boatbuilder from British Columbia wrote asking for a jar of polyestermite tadpoles.

Most disastrous visit to the Royal Yacht *Britannia*

On a visit to Germany, the Queen with Royal guests lined the rails of the *Britannia* to witness an impressive floodlit display including guard of honour and orchestra. According to Andrew Morton (*The Royal Yacht Britannia*, Orbis, 1984) what followed next was definitely not in the schedule.

The conductor, as was the custom, was given the signal from the Monarch to come aboard to receive his thanks for a job well done.

He never made it. In his eagerness to get aboard, he chose the wrong gangplank – the one for the crew – and became hopelessly lost in the company quarters, floundering about in the bowels of the ship.

Sadly he never got to meet the Queen at all.

Best nautical headline

My nomination for this came above a short article from the *Daily Telegraph*'s Rome correspondent in January 1981. The report told how the eleven-man crew of the small Italian merchant ship, the *Giorita*, 927 tons, had jettisoned 500 tons of wine to keep their vessel afloat in heavy seas and 60 m.p.h. gusts off Sardinia.

Two Russian cargo ships and an Italian passenger vessel answered the SOS and, protecting the *Giorita* from the full force of the sea, escorted her into shelter at Olbia after the crew had jettisoned the cargo.

Heading the report was the alluring headline:

'CREW TURN WINE INTO WATER TO SAVE SHIP.'

My runner up in the contest comes also from the *Telegraph* this time in January 1979: 'THREE SAILORS SAVED IN NICK OF TIME'. No, the monster of the deep was not about to engulf them at any moment. Their £12,000 catamaran was named . . . *The Nick of Time*.

Most unexpected request by a helmsman

Storm-tossed sailor Stephen McMullen decided he was 'a goner' as he battled at the helm of the 94ft British ketch *Algaiola* off Bermuda in a hurricane. So he called his girlfriend to the cockpit, and proposed.

Sue Hodgson was amazed to be summoned to the wave-lashed helm for such a purpose, especially as 40ft waves were battering the deck and it was the middle of the night. But she immediately accepted.

'He did propose on bended knee, but that was because he was trying to hold onto the wheel,' said a delighted Miss Hodgson, thirty-one, of Petersfield Hants, in December 1981.

Mr McMullen, thirty, of Chester, said: 'I thought we had had it and that I had better propose while I had the chance.'

The *Algaiola* was helped back to Bermuda by a US coastguard ship through 70 m.p.h. winds as the couple made plans for their honeymoon.

Least royal transatlantic welcome

Single-handed American yachtsman Edward Lormand suffered internal injuries, fought gales and in a 4000-mile epic voyage, was determined to overcome every obstacle to present a gift to the Queen on her Silver Jubilee in 1977.

The forty-one-year-old music professor from Atlanta, Georgia, braved a hurricane, internal bleeding, and spent £23,000 to bring to London his gift of fifty bicentennial dollars and a proclamation from the people of Georgia signed by the Governor.

Despite his injuries sustained two days out from

Florida (which caused him to pass out) and suffering a premature end to his voyage when the rudder of his 28ft glass-fibre sloop *Lormand's 2nd Folly* was smashed on rocks in the Channel Islands, skipper Lormand bravely completed his marathon and inquired of the US Embassy when the Queen would see him to receive his gifts.

He was told that in Silver Jubilee year, her Majesty was far too busy to accept requests such as his, and his gifts would be accepted by a member of the Royal Household instead.

Still gamely he declared: 'I would do the trip again and again for the Queen. It was an honour to sail for her. I would go anywhere – I would even crawl to see her.'

The answer from Buckingham Palace: it's still 'no'.

Ewen Southby-Tailyour

Royal Marines major, Yachtsman of the Year, author . . . and the man who single-handedly charted the Falklands

Favourite memory (1)

It really was a very simple problem. Whilst entering Audierne in Brittany we had fouled the old pilot cutter's propeller with a lobster-pot float. Secretly I believed it served us right for using the engine while we still had a good breeze with plenty of sea room and time; but there we were, motionless.

The skipper did not see the amusing side to the saga despite (to his amazement) the crew bringing the ship to a perfect anchorage under sail. We considered this quite a feat in itself as only the old man and myself had ever sailed before.

Once anchored, the emergency of the past minutes was quickly forgotten as we sat congratulating ourselves over a gin in the cockpit. This luxury was not, however, appreciated by the skipper who glowered with mounting anger as he listened to our light-hearted banter about who should volunteer to plunge into the cool with a diving knife. As it was getting colder and darker, and our run-ashore was in danger of being cancelled, the Irish Parliament of five young Royal Marines officers decided to put off the unwelcome task until the warmth of the next morning's sun.

The discussion became more and more parochial and personal, while it was obvious that none of us wished to draw the short straw, regardless of the time of day. Suddenly we were all shamed into silence as the seventy-year-old skipper stood up, took his glass eye out, placed it carefully on the dog house and jumped overboard with the humiliating shout of 'Call yourselves bloody Commandos'. We were silent for a long time and none of us cared to prepare the dinghy for the shore trip. The moral that we were taught very firmly is that the ship must always be ready for sea regardless of greater attractions. ▶

Favourite memory (2)
I was a reasonably new offshore yacht skipper in the early 1960s and one of my first tasks was to take young officers sail training. We left the Solent area bound for the Helford river. The visibility was not perfect but there was certainly no danger. I had promised the officers a run-ashore in a pub at the end of their first forty-eight hours or so at sea.

I reckoned that the log had been grossly under-reading and so, with all the arrogance of youth, I announced that I knew better, my estimated position was more accurate and that we had nearly run our distance.

With great misplaced confidence I wrote in the log that at such and such a time the Manacle Rocks would appear dead ahead with the Lizard Peninsula stretching away to port in the haze. My orders to the impressed helmsmen were to turn to starboard and the first estuary on the port hand would be Helford. We would be inside the pub inside one hour.

We sighted the rocks (later identified as the Gwineas) with the headland (The Dodman) disappearing southwards into the murk, and gybed to starboard. Instead of finding Nare Head and the river entrance we had sought, we rounded what we eventually knew to be Black Head and went hard aground in St Austell Bay. The log was correct: we were twelve miles short of the distance to run and fifteen degrees off course since rounding, unseen, Prawle Point.

I have preferred sailing without a crew ever since!

Least well-appointed transatlantic craft

Few have tried to make it from England to the West Indies clinging to a wooden plank, but this unusually ill-equipped vessel was the choice of a thirty-two-year-old homesick Jamaican in July 1962.

He had been standing on Hammersmith Bridge musing over the English weather when he decided to make his epic single-handed voyage, scrambling down to the Thames, wading out, and calmly mounting a passing piece of flotsam.

It was at the Star and Garter public house in Putney where astonished regulars spotted – in mid-stream, heading seawards and making a steady three knots – a figure in a floppy hat.

A boat was put out to him but he refused to be rescued. He said: 'I want to stay in the water until I get into the sea, or Jamaica. I want to go home.' But the boat crew insisted and he was hauled aboard.

Most unusual start to sailing training

A nineteen-year-old youth from Swanley, Kent, who admitted stealing a sloop from Burnham, Essex, was said at Essex Quarter Sessions in May 1963 to have 'a fascination for yachting'. The judge kindly sent him to borstal with a recommendation that he should be taught to sail. (No, don't you young folk try it.)

Dick Taverne

Former MP for Lincoln, co-founder of the SDP and QC

Best yachting truism

The entrance to L'Aberwrac'h is, like many approaches in North Brittany, a maze of rocks. In thick fog navigation can be tricky, especially for those who lack sophisticated electronic aids. We had left Roscoff in bright sunshine but long before we got to Ile Vierge lighthouse fog reduced visibility to about fifty yards. We groped our way towards the Libenter buoy which holds the key to the entrance channel. When we thought we should be there and seemed hopelessly lost we suddenly saw another yacht. 'Let's follow them' I cried, and altered course. Then I realized my folly, returned to my previous track and presently heard the buoy, found it, and made my way up the channel.

When we anchored, another boat behind us dropped anchor too. I met the owner ashore. 'I was hopelessly lost,' he said, 'when I saw you pass in the fog. You obviously knew where you were going so we followed you and you got us safely there. Thank you very much.'

Most humiliating cap-in-hand appeal by an old sea dog

It may seem a familiar problem. Boat crazy Leen Verkaik of Amsterdam lavished so much attention on his 45ft yacht (appropriately named *Why Not?*) that his wife gave him something of an ultimatum: it's me or your boat.

He chose the boat, storming out on her to begin in 1981 an epic round-the-world voyage and attempting to prove once and for all that all that varnishing and those never-ending engine repairs were completely worthwhile.

Unfortunately, he made it only as far as the Scillies when his sails became torn and the engines gave up the ghost.

Not only was poor Mr Verkaik, seventy, forced to send an SOS to the Falmouth coastguard, but also a distress signal to his wife, whom he hadn't seen for five years. He said: 'I have to get in touch with her to see if she will send me some money.'

Most unusual lifeboat rescue

A yacht called Sunbird radioed an SOS to the coastguard in June 1986 after being invaded in Chichester harbour by a swarm of bees. As you might imagine, this posed no problem for the ever-ready RNLI who despatched the very man, lifeboatman Simon Wilson – a part-time beekeeper. He said: 'It was just lucky I knew something about bees. I went aboard the yacht and scooped them up with a dustpan and brush. No one was stung.' (No, not even for salvage!)

Ven. William Thomas

Archdeacon of Northumberland and noted sailing enthusiast

Most eventful voyage

You should know that at the time my brother-in-law was vicar of the only RAF station, so far as I know, that is almost entirely underground. Well, chaplain really because it was in his parish. Anyway, this post entitled him to join the RAF Sailing Association which in turn entitled him to hire one of their yachts.

So there we were: two clergymen of the Church of England, one medical general practitioner, one farmer, and one wing-commander RAF (retired) setting sail from the River Hamble on a great adventure.

The next morning, towards the end of the morning watch we were off the Cherbourg Peninsula full and bye on the starboard tack in our 34ft sloop when over the horizon to the west loomed the *Queen Mary* (that dates us!). We calculated that at her rate of knots and our course she would run us down in about five or ten minutes.

'Power gives way to sail!' we said but with little conviction.

'And do you want to put that theory to the test?' said the skipper, a clergyman with his Master's Ticket no less.

'I'll tell you one thing,' he continued, 'and that is that the last thing the Officer of the Watch wants is little boats like us b**ing about in his path. We'll help him most by making our intentions clear and holding course.'

We did, and the *QM* did a dog's leg around our stern, which is nice to be able to talk about all these years later. It was only an hour or two afterwards that motoring into port on a falling tide we ran aground. Lots of Frenchmen shouted incomprehensible things from the quayside and we thought we picked up the word 'reverse'.

'*C'est non possible*,' shouted the skipper. '*Nous n'avons pas un derriere*!'

That particular voyage sticks in my mind too for what must be the ultimate one-upmanship. We were coming into Yarmouth on the I of W and about to come alongside a spanking fresh-painted luxurious 40ft yacht. On deck were two teenage girls, all tight jeans, sweaters and pony-tails.

'Put out some fend-offs!' we yelled.

They scuttled around the deck for a few moments, then stopped. 'Oh bother!' exclaimed one. 'Daddy left the fend-offs on the other yacht.'

Cheekiest call for assistance

A yachtsman whose boat wouldn't start in Torquay harbour had a quite inventive solution. He called the AA, said he was at the quay and suffering 'engine trouble'. Patrolman Ali Ramsden lived up to the efficient image of his association's calling. He rowed out in a rubber dinghy and calmly corrected the fault.

Malcolm Thornton

Conservative MP for Crosby and former River Mersey pilot

Favourite anecdote

The classic 'dark and stormy night' – a Greek ship, overloaded, underpowered with an *excitable* captain. Force 8 NW gale approaching Liverpool docks. On approach the head tug's wire parts and ship lurches towards the river wall. Captain screams to pilot: 'Jesus Christ!' Pilot replies: 'Don't send a boy, this is a man's job!'

Best Royal Navy story

Two RN ships, one outward bound, one homeward, passed in the Bay of Biscay. One hoists the signal for 'We are holding a religious service' plus the second signal for the interrogative, RQ – in other words, a question mark.

An officer on the second ship demanded, 'Yeoman, what's that signal?' 'There is no such signal,' was the reply.

The officer ordered a message to be flashed to the other ship: 'We do not understand your signal.'

The reply was: 'It says, "For God's sake, where are we?" '

Best pilot story

The relationships between pilots and masters is a complex one. But above all, it is important to have absolute trust on both sides. A story told to me by one of my River Mersey colleagues concerned the day he was given a hard time by a ship's captain.

He had piloted the vessel towards the Manchester Ship Canal to the point where the Manchester pilot took over. Going down to meet the Manchester Ship Canal pilot he told the Captain: 'The pilot is rather deaf. You'll have to shout at him.' Meanwhile, with a twinkle in his eye he told the pilot: 'The Captain is rather deaf, you know.'

The two spent the entire journey to the docks at Manchester shouting at each other at the tops of their voices. It is known as the pilot's revenge!

Worst moment

I remember being aboard a South African merchant ship docking at Birkenhead in the mid-70s in seventy-five knot winds. We swung the ship to go head to tide when the line from one of the two tugs was carried away. The second tug held fast but had to get out of the way. Meanwhile we were blown sideways across the River Mersey – straight towards the Princes Landing Stage and the Isle of Man ferry. We had to drop everything and ring emergency full speed to get out of it.

An enterprising photographer from the *Liverpool Echo* took a picture of this drama from the top of the Post and Echo building, and it showed just how close we came. The headline was 'Hurricane hero of the Mersey'.

I was leader of Wirral Borough Council at the time and on entering the council chamber was soon deflated. The leader of the Opposition greeted me with the words: 'Some people will do anything for a headline.'

Most tearful ordeal in a life raft

This came to seven men taking part in the Sydney to Hobart yacht race in 1968 whose boat was overturned by a school of 60ft whales 600 miles off New Zealand. They were successfully rescued by the tanker *British Queen* after being adrift for five days in a rubber life raft. How had they coped in those lonely days and nights, they were asked. Well, said the seven, some of them apparently weeping, we shared the rations. What rations, they were asked. Tears welled up again: 'Four carrots and fourteen onions.'

Favourite Royal Navy story

A RN Corvette overshot the harbour in one north of Scotland port and came to rest with its prow firmly embedded in the coast road. By night, a passing postman just setting off on his rounds was sent cartwheeling over the handlebars when he struck the ship's protruding bow.

'Why don't you show some lights?' he fumed in the direction of the Corvette's bridge.

For one despondent officer, realizing he was on his way to a court martial, this was the end of a long and particularly cruel day.

'Why didn't you ring your friggin' bell,' he shouted back.

World record demand for sea-sickness cures

This came, according to the *Daily Mirror*'s antipodean columnist Michael Parkinson among visitors tripping the six miles out to the America's Cup shenanigans in Fremantle in 1987, and ranged from a run on pills to 'contraptions you strap to your wrist or stick behind your ears'.

'A few people have tried all three,' reported Mr Parkinson, 'and still ended up in the toilet "driving the porcelain bus" as they say hereabouts.'

The result was a happy one – ocean racing was one sport without crowd violence, reported the chat-show host. ('It is very difficult doing damage to your neighbour when he is being seasick.') Mr Parkinson promised on his return to mount a campaign to force British soccer clubs to play all their matches in the North Sea.

The answer why a boat is always a she

One answer, I should say. This one supplied to passengers on an American cruise and reported by *Daily Star* diarist Peter Tory: 'She's all decked out, and it takes a good man to handle her right. She knows her topsides, hides her bottom, and when coming into port, always heads for the buoys.'

Loftiest-ever mayday call

The skipper of a large motor yacht sinking off the eastern United States coast radioed for help and was asked by the coastguard for his position.

Attempting to pull rank he replied: 'I'm executive vice-president of the First National Bank. Please hurry.'

Boat Crazy!

Useful Phrases: A Landlubber-Old Salt Translator

To join the sailing fraternity properly, you must of course become familiar with its unique language. New salts can get away with just two words at first: 'Ahoy' ('Ahoy there', 'Ahoy that buoy' and so on) and 'Athwartships!' (an all-purpose word which immediately qualifies you as an aficionado).

Formerly 'shiver me timbers' might have been added to the above, though seems a bit archaic today, the modern equivalent 'shiver me glass-fibre bottom' not having nearly the same ring to it.

For the convenience of landlubbers and the practised I have constructed this ready guide to nautical terminology:

	Landlubbers' translation	*Sailors' meaning*
Admiralty hitch	MoD shoots itself in foot again	money-saving knot (enabling you to gain purchase)
All in the wind	type of indigestion endemic afloat	type of sail shaking endemic afloat

	Landlubbers' translation	*Sailors' meaning*
Allstanding	excitable male state	shout meaning nobody overboard yet
Awning lanyards	a village near Milton Keynes	bits of string to hold the canvas roof on
Back splice	clever shot in lawn tennis	handy splint in case of back injuries caused by falling off the mizzen masthead, etc.
Baggywrinkle	embarrassing folds in unpressed trousers	way of shrouding your shrouds against sail-chafe
Bagpipe the mizzen	obscure Burns' night ritual	obscure sailing ritual involving box-hauling, haggis and neaps, etc.
Baldheader	elderly sailor type	elderly sailing type
Balsa sandwich	British Rail delicacy	unfortunate result when your craft tries to moor between two others
Beetle	old-fashioned parlour game	old-fashioned mallet used to stop people cheating in old-fashioned parlour games

	Landlubbers' translation	*Sailors' meaning*
Belly halyard	garment worn after hernia op.	extra rope for hauling up gaffs before hernia op.
Bitter end	last sip at closing time	where your ropes stop rotting
Boater	a man (or woman) in a boat	prestigious head adornment seen most at Henley
Bobstay purchase	command by angry wife while dress shopping	nifty bit of tackle required only if you've bought too long a bowsprit
Boom crutch	excitable male state	something to stop a large wooden cylindrical object crashing repeatedly against your head
Bullseye fairlead	expression of appreciation from audience during darts match (see Jim Bowen, p. 17)	oversized bobbin to allow you to haul ropes in, trip and fall overboard, etc.
Bumpkins	the cast of 'The Archers', 'Crossroads," etc.	inexperienced sailor who wouldn't know a baggywrinkle from a clam cleat
Clam cleat	derogatory term for Cambridge oarsmen	handy device to stop you doing an involutary Indian rope trick

	Landlubbers' translation	*Sailors' meaning*
Capstan	strong untipped cigarette	handy seat on the quayside for nosey landlubbers
Carlins	glittering US soap opera	bits of wood which guide you to your cabin late at night
Carrick bend	another pretty village near Milton Keynes	prettiest way to tie two rope ends together if you're tired of granny knots
Caught aback	found doing unmentionable things with an unmarried crew member	doing unmentionable things to an unmarried crew member
Chafing gear	old D-I-Y clothes	old sailing clothes
Cheek block	anything to sit on	a pulley with one end missing
Clove hitch	surfeit of garlic	a granny knot
Coach whipping	ritual flogging after losing in boat race	pretty ways of disgusing clove hitches, grannies, etc.
Dipping lug	hereditary disease of the earlobe	funny sort of sail tapered at one end
Fiddle	claim social security, etc, while working	bits of plywood stuck to tables etc., to make things tip up instead of sliding off

	Landlubbers' translation	*Sailors' meaning*
Flukes	unexpected win at cards	bits of the end of an anchor or nasty dose or worms.
Foul hawse	derogatory upper-class description of working-class home	a sort of sailing whiplash when a ship gets all tied up in itself
Four bells	two large whiskies	passing on the first dog watch (as if you'd see many dogs floating out at sea)
Futtock plank	a kind of wooden seat	an obscure broad plank near to the keel
Gaff	unfortunate mistake much pioneered by sports commentators, etc.	a spar (non-supermarket variety) to which the head of a fore-and-aft sail is crooked (honest!)
Garboard strake	seafood delicacy	another obscure broad-in-the-beam plank next to the keel
Gimbals	a long-running cartoon strip in the *Daily Express*	an object for keeping light level so you can read long-running cartoon strips in the *Daily Express*

	Landlubbers' translation	*Sailors' meaning*
Girth band	large belt	something you sew into your sail when it's putting on weight
Gore strake	Australian expletive	translated: 'tough luck'. Means boatyard men taking industrial action
Griping spar	device for babies to cut their teeth on	very annoyed bit of wood
Hanging knee	scene of famous Australian film, i.e., 'Picnic at . . .'	a famous eighteenth-century captain who liked to pass the death penalty on recalcitrants
Hard chine	Australian term of commiseration	a lot of bright-work to polish on the outside of your boat
Harp piece	strident feminists	the extreme part of a sailing vessel which may be kicked in anger
Highfield lever	another village near Milton Keynes	sort of onboard crank (as if there aren't enough of those)
Hobby horsing	playing with model railway engines	playing with boat engines

	Landlubbers' translation	*Sailors' meaning*
Hove to	ancient instruction as in 'Dewsbury to', 'Cleethorpes to'	ancient instruction as in 'Falmouth to, or Dover, to'
Jackstay	wife's command when husband about to leave for pub	means of tying up sails to stop them falling off
Jury rig	ancient Old Bailey custom	frequent sailing custom after mast breaks in two, etc.
Kedge anchor	well-known brand of butter	expensive means of holing a yacht's dinghy
Keelson topping	cream substitute used for dressing trifles, etc.	another village near Milton Keynes
King plank	revered South Pacific monarch	line on deck defying sailors to walk straight along
King spoke	ancient monarchical greeting	chewed protruberance on ship's wheel
Leading cleat	most unpopular member of a pub outing	most unpopular member of a boat's crew
Lee Helmsman Lee Lurch Lee Marvin	well-known Hollywood actors	unfortunate sailing aberrations having gathered too much wind

	Landlubbers' translation	*Sailors' meaning*
List	written note, e.g., to take shopping	written note, e.g., to take to chandlers
Luff	endearment, e.g., 'From Russia with Luff'	the chewed-up bit of your sails
Marina	Morris car with not the same style as say, a Morris Minor	large expensive car park for boats
Mariner	well-known footballer	sailor who has served his ten years in (a) the Royal Navy (b) the Merchant Navy (c) the *Hope and Stanley Knife*
Mast partners	a couple who got on well during a sailing holiday	a couple who got on well during a sailing holiday
Matthew Walker	a brand of ale much loved in the Manchester area	upmarket name for a granny knot
Merriman clips	comedian from the Northern club circuit	fast-opening shackle much used by stunt men, sailors, bondage freaks, etc.
Midshipman hitch	marriage, e.g., between HRH Prince Andrew and Miss Sarah Ferguson	yet another fanciful knot

	Landlubbers' translation	*Sailors' meaning*
Missed stays	unfortunate loss of corsets	unfortunate loss of wind
Monkey's fist	mess, e.g., 'You've made a right money's fist out of that.'	fiercest of all granny knots
Mud flats	three traditionally constructed council estates in east London	most common disembarking place for new sailors
Mule sail	donkey on paddleboat in Peasholm Park	any voyage where the skipper has made an ass of himself
Oakum	a town in what used to be called Rutland	frayed rope covered in tar (not recommended for flagellation)
Oil bag	derogatory term for unwelcome colleague	derogatory term for unwelcome member of crew
Parbuckle	a large boil, often on the foot	device for getting big cylindrical objects (nothing rude though) aboard
Pilot books	a captain flying with Dan Air	essential if incomprehensible yachting version of AA book
Planking clamp	rare sexually transmitted disease	a tool used to keep your plank against the rib (honest!)

	Landlubbers' translation	*Sailors' meaning*
Plummer block	rare form of amnesia	a shaft bearing which is either roller or friction type while housing bolts to a horizontal surface (honest!)
Polyvinyl alcohol	desperate shore tipple	desperate yachting tipple
Pontoon	a card game	large floating protruberance for crashing into at speed
Poop deck	unusual hand in a card game	raised part of boat where guests can walk dogs late at night
Port hole	mouth of fortified wine drinking person	device for quickly flooding ship if left ajar
Pudden fender	well-loved dessert	large cowcatcher device at the bow for crashing into other vessels with
Ram bow	fictional film character played by Sylvester Stallone	large below waterline device at the bow for crashing into other vessels with
Rockered	ancient expression for extreme tiredness	a boat which is 'bent' in the non-Old Bailey jury sense

	Landlubbers' translation	*Sailors' meaning*
Rudder trunk	slipping complaint of the abdomen caused by excessive imbibing	hole in the boat's stern through which the rudder (with luck) is attached
Sailmaker's whipping	another well-loved cream substitute for desserts, etc.	'the best of all whipping' – genuine testimonial in array of sailing and sado-masochism books
Sextant	man in charge of graveyard	expensive-looking navigational aid (not as expensive as some navigators though)
Silicon bronze	type of sun-tan oil much favoured by well-endowed ladies	alloy used for making boat nails
Sister Hook	famous convent habituée (daughter of Captain Hook)	way of joining ropes together without a granny
Snap shackle	lock on lunch container	openable, adjustable metal granny
Spike bowsprit	well-loved ticket tout from London	combined bowsprit and jib
Split backstay	embarrassing hole in corsets	embarrassing hole in trousers

	Landlubbers' translation	*Sailors' meaning*
Spurling pipe	a wine bar in Covent Garden.	usual nickname for well-known part of a sailor's anatomy
Standing lug	a disease of the outer ear	almost the same as dipping lug though not quite as dangerous
Stove in	expression of satisfaction at new kitchen equipment	expression of satisfaction at new galley equipment
Swinging the compass	obtaining doctor's note, etc., by deception	ancient water-borne ritual after heavy shore drinking session
TBT	an international courier firm always advertising on TV	a banned paint which kills marine life, crustaceans, swimmers, etc.
Taffrail	the commuter train network around Cardiff	rails to prevent people popping off the poop
Talurit splice	type of ice-cream sundae	soft metal collar much loved by sado-masochists
Tar epoxy	expression of gratitude	extremely sticky resin for messing up, fingers, arms, hair, etc.

	Landlubbers' translation	*Sailors' meaning*
Throat halyard	a woman's necklace	the tackles used to hoist the throat end of the gaffer (nothing to do with hanging the skipper from the yardarm, though)
Toe rail	another expression of contempt	another device to stop people falling off the boat
Trochoidal wave	disease of the throat akin to tonsilitis	friendly greeting to crew of another boat
Truss frame	vital equipment after hernia op.	means of giving boat-builders etc. hernia op.
Under canvas	failure by political party to doorstep enough voters	night on board after too much reefing, sails having fallen on top of you
West Country whipping	another imitation cream dessert delight	on board entertainment much favoured by gentlemen of a certain age
Wild Dee Shackles	country and western singer from Halifax	objects necessary to secure the above
Wild gybe	unfortunate (and failed) attempt at humour (no, you surely don't mean this book!)	attempt at getting the best out of sailing (no, you surely don't mean this book!)

About the Author

Actually his first name is David, but he got fed up with jokes about lockers. Graham Jones ('Jonah' to his enemies) is a Fleet Street journalist and the author of a number of humorous books, his previous work being *The Official Candidates' Book of Political Insults* (Century, 1987). He was born in 1951 in that well-known seafaring port, Halifax, Yorks., later moving to Wakefield where as a boy he watched the big boats on the Aire and Calder Navigation: so it is not surprising it has taken him thirty-six years to get round to writing about life afloat. He has some experience of boats, mostly crashing them into others, and he did gather a crowd on one famous occasion as he tried to make a three-point turn on the River Bure in a sailing dinghy.

He says he would like to list his hobby as messing about in boats, but the truth is he would mess about wherever he was.

Also by Graham Jones

FORKED TONGUES
OWN GOALS
THE FORKED TONGUES ANNUAL
I DON'T HATE MEN/WOMEN BUT . . .
PLANE CRAZY
THE OFFICIAL CANDIDATES' BOOK OF POLITICAL INSULTS